ATHLETE HABITS

8 FUNDAMENTAL HABITS THAT ELITE ATHLETES CULTIVATE TO REACH AND MAINTAIN SUCCESS

HADLEY MANNINGS

© Copyright 2020 - All rights reserved.

The content contained within this book may not be reproduced, duplicated or transmitted without direct written permission from the author or the publisher.

Under no circumstances will any blame or legal responsibility be held against the publisher, or author, for any damages, reparation, or monetary loss due to the information contained within this book, either directly or indirectly.

Legal Notice:

This book is copyright protected. It is only for personal use. You cannot amend, distribute, sell, use, quote or paraphrase any part, or the content within this book, without the consent of the author or publisher.

Disclaimer Notice:

Please note the information contained within this document is for educational and entertainment purposes only. All effort has been executed to present accurate, up to date, reliable, complete information. No warranties of any kind are declared or implied. Readers acknowledge that the author is not engaged in the rendering of legal, financial, medical or professional advice. The content within this book has been derived from various sources. Please consult a licensed professional before attempting any techniques outlined in this book.

By reading this document, the reader agrees that under no circumstances is the author responsible for any losses, direct or indirect, that are incurred as a result of the use of the information contained within this document, including, but not limited to, errors, omissions, or inaccuracies.

CONTENTS

SPECIAL BONUS!	v
Introduction	vii
1. Develop a Plan	1
2. Be Consistent and Focused	15
3. Visualization and Mental Training	31
4. Sleep, Rest, and Recover	52
5. Healthy Eating to Fuel Your Body	71
6. Improve Your Awareness	87
7. Build Your Network	109
8. Believe in Yourself	123
Conclusion	145
One Last Thing Before You Go...	151
References	153

SPECIAL BONUS!

Thank for you purchasing Athlete Habits! Get this additional book about Athlete Motivation 100% FREE!

Many others have already received this free book as well as other full length books—all 100% free! If you want insider access plus Athlete Motivation, scan the QR code below with your smartphone camera.

INTRODUCTION

CITIUS - ALTIUS - FORTIUS

THE OLYMPIC MOTTO

These Latin words translate to "faster - higher - stronger."

You don't have to be an Olympic athlete to want to become faster and stronger. You don't need to be an Olympic athlete to want to perform better in your sport. You certainly don't have to be an Olympic athlete to learn from other Olympic and professional athletes and borrow some of their training techniques.

Different athletes have different habits, and different practices have varying degrees of success for different people.

The greatest sprinter of all time, Jamaica's Usain Bolt, certainly has habits that have propelled him to greatness. His swagger and comedic antics at the starting line work for him.

Michael Phelps also has highly effective habits, but his approach to beginning a race looks very different from Bolt's. He sits down. He listens to music and has a much more cerebral and contemplative approach.

It doesn't matter which athlete you identify with or your current level of athletic performance—learning about the best of the best and what makes them that way will open up pathways to improve yourself.

WHO IS THIS BOOK FOR?

If you want to be on top of your game every day, this book is for you.

If you are frustrated by spending time and effort searching for answers and information to help your athletic development, this book is for you.

If you want to see beyond the trendy diets, gimmicks, and the trendy fads in working out, this book is for you.

If you don't want one approach pushed upon you, but would rather have several options that are tested and vetted by professional athletes presented to you—so that you can choose which is best for you—this book is for you.

This book is for athletes with significant levels of experience, upcoming young athletes who have lots of potentials, people who want to take their local game to the next level, or are people who are just getting started.

Coaches and trainers will find cutting edge insight

into methods and effective habits for optimizing sports performance.

For those athletes, coaches, and trainers who have been focusing primarily on physical training, this book might open your mind to the authentic power of mental training for athletes.

According to the science behind the practice of yoga, the body only executes activities. The activities all originate inside the athlete's mind.

When athletes compete, the split-second decisions and responses to external activity are critical. The most complex piece of athletic performance is the correct identification of signals and the selection, production, and on-the-spot improvisation of accurate responses.

Think about how complex that is. These things don't just happen.

The development of healthy mental habits allows the athlete's mind to access memories and hopes for the future to enable the correct response to emerge.

Athletes who tap into the power of mental training take advantage of this competitive edge.

Unfortunately, athletes that only focus on the physical aspects of training do not have access to this untapped potential.

WHAT IS THIS BOOK ABOUT?

Athletes need to have the mindset of a warrior to succeed. All human beings need to excel, but athletes are different.

Athletic competition is born from this need. Throughout history, warriors fought and battled against one another to prove their superiority. As civilization advanced, the need for this competition and battle emerged in the form of competitive sports. However, the need to compete behind the struggle and the pride of victory remains the same.

Due to this link between sports and battle, competition and the need to emerge victoriously relate to killer instincts. Focus, split-second decision making, and precise execution are all required in war and, of course, in athletics. To achieve this kind of performance requires self-control of thoughts, emotions, behaviors, and habits.

In sports, we all know that the better player does not always win—the player who plays better wins.

Athletes who consistently win can never sit back and relax. Just because they have always won or usually win does not mean they will continue to win.

The opposite is also true. Teams that consistently lose will not lose forever.

Athletes that understand the eight fundamentals habits required to improve have a genuine chance of becoming champions.

Although winners and losers are often determined mainly by physical prowess, everyday habits and training of the mind can ignite personal athletic growth.

This book proves that adopting habits used by other successful athletes is critical for every aspiring athlete who wants to improve their game. You'll find many examples of top athletes who use these habits, so you know they have **credibility**.

WHAT CAN PEOPLE TAKE AWAY FROM THIS BOOK?

When you finish reading this book, you will have learned practical steps that are realistic for anyone to take to adopt and benefit from these eight habits.

You will learn simple, meaningful, and practical strategies and habits to develop athletic performance. Whether you are looking to run faster, jump higher, throw farther, or improve your overall approach to your sport and yourself as an athlete, this book is for you.

When athletes train and compete without a roadmap, they leave the potential for great achievement on the table. Great athletes research best practices and follow the advice from athletic thought leaders to achieve continuous progress in their field.

With this book and the habits within, you will walk away with a roadmap that will lead you to results you may never have thought you could have achieved.

With practice, persistence, and commitment, you will achieve results.

CHAPTER ONE

DEVELOP A PLAN

DEVELOPING a plan helps athletes improve their capacity to focus their energy. Focusing on planning and goals helps athletes develop habits that govern emotions, thought processes, and actions.

Goals might involve developing and cultivating better habits or breaking harmful and unwanted habits.

Designing goals that boost motivation is critical for improvement. Athletes should ask themselves what it is that truly motivates them to want to set goals and achieve outcomes. Doing so reinforces an athlete's commitment and taps into the inner drive that sustains the athlete through the bad times and the good.

Athletes need the will to face hardships and endure the challenges that lie ahead. They need the discipline to build stamina and avoid distractions. Being powered and fueled by clearly identified inner desires will enable athletes to plan and set appropriately challenging and achievable goals.

WHAT IS GOAL SETTING FOR ATHLETES?

When Michael Phelps was eight years old, he wrote a list of goals. The goal that topped the list was Phelps' dream to make the Olympics. Well, we all know how that turned out.

His goals don't stop there. Throughout his career, Phelps also set goals for his season. For each racing event, he set smaller short-term goals for the beginning, middle, and end of his season.

Research shows that when we take the extra few minutes to write down our goals, we increase our chances of achieving success by 33% (Price-Mitchell, 2018).

Goal setting is the process of leveraging your core values about success in your particular sport to evaluate your performance and achieve your personal best.

HOW SHOULD ATHLETES SET GOALS?

For many years, people have used the acronym SMART to set goals in all areas of life, from personal and professional to educational and athletic goals.

The acronym stands for Specific, Measurable, Attainable, Relevant, and Time-Bound. When it comes to athletic performance, here are what SMART goals look like for athletes:

Specific – Professional athletes and their trainers

use specific goals, and so should you. Specific goals enable athletes to hold themselves accountable. You can't say if you're pitching more accurately, but you can tell if you are throwing first-pitch strikes with more frequency.

A simple formula to ensure the goal is specific enough: I will [state goal] by [doing what? How often? When?].

Measurable – When goals are measurable, athletes can quantifiably evaluate progress toward reaching those goals. If Michael Phelps' time on the breaststroke weren't progressing in the middle of his season towards the goal he set, it would alert him that something wasn't working. He could then redirect his training regimen or make other adjustments.

Attainable – Goals, of course, should be sufficiently challenging and above your current level of play and performance. They should push you from your comfort zone and require a real commitment. At the same time, goals should be attainable. Attainable goals are possible to achieve. Unrealistic setting goals can cause confidence setbacks, which are good for no one. Work with a growth mindset that seeks to move the needle. If you are someone who makes free shots 40% of the time, a 55% goal is more realistic than a 75% goal. You can always adjust the goal to make it more challenging along the way. Wouldn't that feel great?

Relevant – A relevant goal aims to take you from where you are to where you want to go. Objective assessments of gap analysis drive relevant goals. This assessment should be a combination of self-assessment and feedback from coaches and data. Motivational speakers like Tony Robbins have been wildly successful at encouraging goal setting because they understand people and what makes them tick. One strategy that Tony Robbins encourages others to adopt is what he calls the "pull strategy." Besides focusing on what you have to do, Robbins recommends reframing that behavior to become motivated by what you want to do. For example, going out for a run is a push strategy because it's part of your regular workout routine. Pull strategy reframes that run to propel you toward a meaningful goal of scoring more runs for your team. Robbins says, "The person who is motivated by necessity is interested in what's known and what's secure. The person who is motivated by possibility is equally interested in what's not known. He wants to know what can evolve, what opportunities might develop" (Ward, n.d.).

Time-bound – Adding a timeline for accomplishing milestones and goals increase the likelihood that you will stay on track and achieve your goals. An approaching deadline helps athletes maintain the self-discipline required to do whatever it takes to achieve that goal. For example, athletes might complete early morning training sessions or skip social activities to get in additional practice.

Below are a few examples of goals developed using the **SMART** framework:

By the first day of gameplay, [TIME-BOUND]

I will throw first-pitch strikes [SPECIFIC]
to eight of ten batters [MEASUREABLE].

The wording in the goal won't necessarily tell us if the goal is ATTAINABLE or RELEVANT. To ensure that your goals meet these criteria, try to be introspective, and consult with a coach to ensure the goals are appropriately set.

WHY DO ATHLETES SET GOALS?

A national championship field hockey coach strongly believed that a successful goal-scoring play must include **ten successful passes** before the shot on goal is taken. The coach put more emphasis on the passing game than on the goal itself.

The game transformed quickly. Players quickly adjusted their position to get themselves open and ready to receive the ball. The player in possession focused on passing and getting into a position to receive again. The coach loudly counted the passes to encourage the team. With each pass, the team remained focused on the passing game and never favored any particular player to score a quick goal.

Did they regularly pass ten times? No. In fact, at first, their scoring numbers decreased.

However, as the team gelled under this strategy, they gained momentum, scoring more, and ultimately winning the national championship. Wins were satisfying for every player.

Ten passes' short-term goal provided a laser-specific

strategy that created focus and enthusiasm among the team and each player.

Goal setting provides many benefits for athletes:

Sustains Motivation and Focus

Athletes should use historical data to design attainable short-term goals that align with long-term goals. These short-term goals will motivate athletes to continue their pursuit of long-term goals. When this happens, the athlete is likely to sustain and even increase their focus and train even harder.

Improves Performance

Athletes who are driven by goals are more likely to concentrate on the task at hand. The focus is on the process rather than the outcome.

Some athletes use goals to focus on the here-and-now of their training. For example, a runner might repeat a mantra associated with the goal. A cyclist might focus on smooth and efficient pedaling by imagining the wheels of a steam train.

When athletes focus on goals and the process associated with achieving them, they can ignore the outcome, which can be overwhelming and instead concentrate specifically on the task.

When athletes dedicate their attention to the present moment, that attention tends to be quite powerful. This focus can significantly increase the likelihood of achieving that process goal.

Provides a Calming Effect

Past mistakes and failures tend to creep into the memory and cause the same errors to occur repeatedly—this may lead to a fear of the future. Fretting over the past and fearing the future are two unwanted behaviors that must be incorporated when athletes consider goal planning.

Creating a goal to focus on excellence and honoring it will reduce these two unwanted behaviors. It will also provide a calming effect. A goal like this can trigger you to produce excellence whenever you see it.

Knowing that a plan is in place to manage overall athletic performance leads to decreased stress and anxiety in the mind of the athlete. Goals can be soothing reminders that assist in achieving the desired outcome.

The athlete can relax at the end of the day, knowing that everything that they could have done has been done to achieve the best possible outcome. Without well-designed goals, the question of "What if?" can cause unnecessary stress during less-than-perfect practice and competition.

Encourages Self-Improvement

Setting goals results in improved athletic performance, but the byproducts of setting, measuring, and achieving goals is immensely valuable. Athletes benefit from the boost in self-confidence that comes from achieving goals. Also, focusing on personal goals nurtures the positive habits that focus on the athlete rather than comparing the athlete to others.

Impacts Perception About the Future

When athletes set goals, they are tapping into their ability to affect their future positively. Setting and achieving goals helps the athlete remember that they do have control over their performance. This feeling is called an internal locus of control. Studies show that people with an internal locus of control believe that their actions and skills determine success, and they have more positive feelings about how their efforts impact the outcome.

HOW SHOULD ATHLETES SET GOALS?

Imagine a mountain climber who has a long-term goal of completing a climb. Strategically designed short-term goals are crucial to achieving the long-term goal.

When setting goals, today's practice should be considered just as important as the ultimate competition. Giving equal weight to short-term and long-term goals is critical.

Short-Term Goals

Short-term goals are those that can be achieved within a short period and provide immediate feedback.

Short-term goals can help athletes remain grounded and focused as they endure the moment-to-moment struggles involved with intense training and competition.

Rather than focusing on uncontrollable factors like the score or the overall team performance, short-term goals refocus the athlete's attention to items over which they do have control. When athletes identify elements over which they have power and use those elements to design short-term goals, they can concentrate on energy, which can significantly influence the result.

Athletes can use short-term goals in a single session or a series of sessions. Short-term goals help to maintain forward momentum and establish the foundation for achieving long-term goals. Short-term goals should include actionable and measurable milestones that align with long-term goals.

Considering that achievement is motivational, short-term goals provide athletes with a sense of accomplishment that conditions the mind to see goals as challenges instead of obstacles.

Following a few simple steps will make establishing short-term goals easy and attainable.

Begin with the end in mind. Begin with the end goal in mind, continue to work backward, and drill it down to be as specific as possible in the short-term. If a baseball player who is currently batting .280 has a long-term goal to bat .300 by the end of the season, that player should work backward and begin by asking "What would it take for me to achieve this long-term goal?" Finding the answer will lead to the right short-term goals. More batting practice is good. Fifteen minutes per day of additional batting practice is better. Drilling down all the way, however, will result in a better outcome. For example, if data shows the player has trouble hitting the curveball, a short-term goal should be designed to address that particular pain point.

Be specific. No item is too specific. Goals surrounding analytics, work ethic, rest, attitude, prompt attendance, and performance during warm-ups can be meaningful if appropriately designed. A short-term goal for the baseball player in the above example may be to obtain data from coaching staff and spend an hour per week analyzing areas for improvement.

Use positive phrasing. When designing goals, positively phrased goals are more motivational than negatively phrased goals. For example, a negative goal like "commit fewer fouls" can be rephrased as "complete five foul-free minutes of scrimmage play." Athletes can then focus on achieving success rather than eliminating failure.

Examples of short-term goals include:

- Increase weights by 5% every week.
- Practice free throws for 20 minutes five times per week.
- Spend an additional 10 minutes in the cages per practice hitting curveballs.

Long-Term Goals

Long-term goals are the driving force behind why you play, compete, practice, and participate in your sport. Most people underestimate what they can achieve in the long term.

There are a few different types of goals. It's important to understand the different types as you design your long-term goals since different types have different degrees of success and affect athletes and their performance.

Outcome goals - Outcome goals refer to winning and losing. Athletes have little control over these goals.

Performance goals - Performance goals refer to independent athlete performance as it applies to their standards for excellence. Here, athletes have much more control as this type of goal only measures their performance.

Process goals - Process goals refer to the proficiency an athlete demonstrates in performing a particular skill, technique, or strategy. For example, in basketball free throws, the skill might be achieving an arc on the throw. In baseball, the batting skill might be keeping the player's head still while swinging the bat.

All of these goals are important in developing an athlete's overall skills. Still, studies show that athletes who concentrate on process and performance goals benefit from the process of goal setting more than those who focus on outcome goals. These athletes also reported better athletic performance, felt more confident, focused, and satisfied, and were less anxious.

Make no mistake. As athletes work towards long-term goals, there will be failure along the way.

Yankees legend Derek Jeter often says that the path to success isn't always about winning. Jeter said one of the best qualities about coach Joe Torre was his calm and supportive demeanor. Believe it or not, Jeter made mistakes. Torre encouraged him to keep swinging for the fences instead of becoming too cautious.

Jeter always respected Torre for allowing him to fail because it also allowed him to succeed.

THE GOALS ARE ESTABLISHED. NOW WHAT?

Once short and long-term goals have been properly established, the process is long from over. If goals are used effectively, they are used as part of an ongoing process that includes the following steps:

Reevaluation

Depending on the situation, athletes should review the progress made to maintain focus and sustain momentum. Although still effective if done independently, athletes should perform this evaluation with a coach, mentor, or teammate.

Perhaps goal difficulty was miscalculated, and athletes need to adjust goals that were too easily achieved or too challenging.

Progress recognition and encouragement

Again, even if the athlete performs this exercise independently, it can be very effective. An athlete can reward themselves with a massage or a new piece of training equipment once milestones are achieved. Coaches who publicly or privately recognize athletes as they progress toward goals provide motivation.

Acknowledge and evaluate obstacles

For many athletes, obstacles will arise during the pursuit of long-term goals. Whether athletes experience a physical plateau, a lack of confidence, or problems balancing other commitments, the key is to identify and acknowledge these obstacles and develop strategies to deal with them.

Goal progress feedback and evaluation

Having some level of accountability to an external source seems to be effective in maintaining confidence and motivation.

Research found that when external feedback is added to the goal achievement process, significantly higher performance - 17% higher - was the result.

POINTS TO REMEMBER

- Developing a plan helps athletes develop the capacity to focus their energies.
- Taking the extra few minutes to write down goals increases the chances of achieving success.
- Goals should be SMART: Specific, Measurable, Attainable, Relevant, and Time-Bound.
- Giving equal weight to short-term and long-term goals is critical.
- For goals to be used effectively, they must be used and reevaluated as part of an ongoing process.

CHAPTER TWO

BE CONSISTENT AND FOCUSED

CONSISTENCY

EVERYONE IS after the ideal performance state. The self-improvement industry exists because of this elusive desire.

Athletes are no different.

When athletes are in the ideal performance state, they feel mentally and physically focused and confident that they will perform at a level of personal excellence.

Talk to athletes. They will tell you that when they have performed particularly well, they have been confident, focused, and completely immersed in the present moment. It's that feeling of 'flow' when every piece of the puzzle fits perfectly in place.

To achieve flow during a competition, athletes must do everything to put themselves on 'autopilot' by trusting their practice and training to take over. For this to happen, consistency must be utilized when developing a training regimen.

Most athletes have heard about the importance of being consistent. But the concept can often be too vague to be meaningful. When athletes think about consistency, they might wonder:

- What exactly does that mean?
- Do all repetitive behaviors count? Aren't some just superstitious?
- What behaviors should I be considering?
- Will it make a difference in my athletic performance?

Research about consistency reports on closed skills such as a golf putt, a baseball swing, or a basketball free throw. The bottom line is that athletes who utilize strategies that reinforce consistency enjoy improved performance.

Recycling

For athletes and everyone else, one thing is for sure. Everybody makes mistakes.

However, when athletes make a mistake in competition, it is critically important to let it go immediately. These skills can be learned and practiced to ensure they are consistently applied.

When an athlete is not performing well and becomes frustrated, the wheels fall off, making it very difficult to recover. However, athletes that find themselves not performing well can draw upon consistent strategies to pull themselves back up to avoid frustration. They may find their way to a very different outcome.

Athletes should examine their performance to identify the most common situations where they encounter difficulty and practice working through such situations during training exercises. Practicing these coping skills will develop positive habits that will result in positive reactions to mistakes and poor overall levels of play. When the athlete learns these recycling skills during training, they can transfer them to perform during competition.

Athletes who have not consistently practiced recycling skills during practice are likely to overcompensate for mistakes or poor performance and get into even deeper trouble.

An athlete who consistently lets go of a mistake returns immediately to the task at hand and maintains confidence and composure will have an exponentially greater result than one who does not.

Simulation Training

Simulation training sometimes called adversity training, is a strategy that replicates key elements of competition, which can often be adversarial. For example, football, soccer, or rugby teams will simulate stadium noise in advance of a, particularly competitive match. Practicing amid such conditions prepares athletes to face the conditions in real-time and maintain concentration.

Research suggests that an athlete's recall of information is facilitated by conditions that look, sound, and feel like those where the original training took place. Two primary benefits will often result from simulation training.

- **Positive transfer benefits.** When athletes replicate the environment they expect to compete in during their practice, they can expect to enjoy positive transfer benefits.
- **Improved concentration.** Another advantage of simulation training is its tendency to help athletes maintain focus and decrease the likelihood that unexpected events will distract during competition.

A famous example of simulation training involves Michael Phelps. His coach, Bob Bowman, was infamous for confiscating or breaking Phelps' goggles during practice to train Phelps to maintain concentration without clear goggles. Believe it or not, Phelps' goggles broke during an event in the 2008 Olympics. For the last 100 meters of the race, Phelps swam with broken goggles and won the gold medal.

Pre Performance Routines

Athletics are heavily ritualized. Successful athletes have realized that consistently engaging in preparatory rituals promote excellent performance.

- A player about to shoot a foul shot or serve a tennis ball bounces the ball a certain number of times.
- A softball or baseball player takes three practice swings and might touch the plate before getting into a ready position.
- A golfer might ensure the tag writing on their ball is lined up with the hole before taking a putt.

These rituals are called pre-performance routines. Athletes typically perform such routines just before competing in a self-paced activity that happens independently at the athlete's pace and without external interference.

Pre-performance routines improve concentration because they enable athletes to:

- Remain laser-focused in the present moment. The sequential and repetitive nature of a routine requires concentration to quiet thoughts about past performance or future outcomes.
- Pay complete attention to a specific action over which they have significant control. By paying attention to task-relevant information,

the distraction of other irrelevant stimuli can be minimized.
- Ignore - and even block out - otherwise distracting external activity and thoughts. Paying total attention to one step of a routine after another requires the athlete to focus the entirety of their mental effort. In doing so, appropriate subconscious thoughts can arise in stressful situations to suppress negative thoughts.

Although these pre-performance routines provide a substantial improvement in intentional and attentional behavior, they are sometimes viewed as superstitious. However, it is important to differentiate between pre-performance routines and superstitious behavior.

A tennis player who needs their water jug in the same place on the court and facing in a certain direction before a match is not employing pre-performance routines, they are employing superstition. This qualifies as superstitious behavior since this activity is not logically or rationally causal in the athlete's performance outcome.

Pre-performance routines can be proven to influence the outcome because they enable the athlete to exert control over preparation, skill, strength, focus, etc.

The individual characteristics of the athlete should drive the structure and composition of the routine. For example:

- Stage of learning and experience

- Skill level
- Mental and physical characteristics
- Coping resources
- Situational variables

Also important in designing a pre-performance routine is the desired task-specific performance outcome. There should be a clear relationship between the pre-performance routine and its functionality. For example, if a golfer is incorporating the process of looking at the flag before a tee shot, there should be a specific reason behind such behavior. Perhaps the golfer is working on the task-specific goal of a more accurately directed shot.

Pre-performance rituals that generate peak performance have these characteristics:

- They are consistent. Research shows that elite golfers do the same thing in the same order with the same timing.
- They are used regardless of the situation. Whether trailing or leading by a large differential or a small one, research shows that elite golfers who never fail to practice their routine – every single time in every situation - gain an edge over highly competent golfers who practice their routine less consistently.
- They are planned for specific situations. Situation specific stress, when anticipated, can be overcome with a pre-performance

ritual. Efforts should be concentrated on reducing the tensions that can manifest during competition.

Motivation

One area that is particularly hard to remain consistent in is motivation. Consistent and repetitive training can't happen without motivation.

Athletes and trainers can optimize motivation with the following suggestions.

Be aware of motivation drains. Particularly tough physical, mental, and emotional training sessions can threaten to decrease motivation significantly. The same is true for poor performance during competition or even excellent performance. This resulted in a loss because of an external circumstance like a bad call by an official.

Sustain motivation mid-season. It's natural for motivation to be high at the start of a season and wane as the season goes on. If properly designed and executed, goal setting should pay attention to maintaining motivation and include steps for doing so.

When Things Go Wrong

Maintaining consistency when up against a formidable opponent or while losing is everything.

What happens when things go wrong?

During the 2012 Olympic soccer finals in London, Mexico was up against the team expected to win, Brazil.

Brazil was the reigning Olympic soccer champion. On paper, they were by far the best team.

Mexico, on the other hand, was not expected to put up much of a fight. But they did.

Mexico went to Brazil in an incredible display in the finals. Brazil's players lost their composure. Fans watched in shock as the Brazil players hung their heads. They had not expected things to go this way.

Mexico ended up winning.

Maintaining consistency and avoiding overconfidence requires planning and even practice.

FOCUS

- What does it mean to focus?
- What benefits come from focusing?
- How do elite athletes stay extremely focused?

Imagine the focus a soccer goalkeeper must maintain to protect the goal during the opposing team's corner kick. The goalkeeper must maintain laser-focused on the incoming ball's flight path and tune out multiple distractions, including the movement of the players, noise, doubts, etc.

How can athletes focus on the most important components of practice and competition while at the same time blocking out internal and external distractions?

The answer is focus. When we focus, we exert

mental energy to concentrate only on the external events happening around us and internal thoughts in our minds that are productive in accomplishing specific goals for successful athletic performance.

Poor performance often results from a small mistake. In many cases, that small mistake can be attributed to a lack of focus. The good news is that with dedication and practice, athletes can easily develop and strengthen their ability to focus.

Researchers acknowledge the importance of maintaining focus and have been studying it for years. Sports psychologists have studied strategies that improve athletic focus. Different strategies have different rates of success, depending on the sport and the athlete, of course. Still, they all aim to support a state of mind that is focused on peak performance.

Recognize When You're Getting In Your Own Way

Being able to focus is one thing. Focusing in the right way and on the right things is another.

When athletes focus on themselves and their performance too intensely or for too long, they can experience analysis paralysis. Being able to recognize when this, or any problem associated with maintaining focus, is happening is an important first step to rectifying it.

Human beings are motivated by one of two things in everything they do. They either try to achieve pleasure or avoid pain.

Believe it or not, athletes are sometimes afraid to succeed. Your brain can sometimes subconsciously link pain with success.

Why would the brain do such a thing?

The human brain does not work logically. It works based on association. If you've never been successful in your sport, success is an unknown factor. The brain understands the status quo. The status quo makes the brain feel comfortable. In contrast, the brain also often associates the unknown with pain.

Make sure to check yourself and ensure that your brain is not self-sabotaging.

How can you do this?

- Condition your brain to expect success.
- Develop beliefs that you are capable and worthy of success.
- Know that you already have everything you need to become successful. Train your mind to know it's there for the taking.
- Recognize the abundant nature of the resources available to you since lack attracts lack and abundance attracts abundance.
- Try to acknowledge that we are all equal in our opportunities, but where we differ is decision making, education, motivation, empowering beliefs, and how much we demand from each other and ourselves.

Set Performance Goals

We discussed the importance of goal setting in the previous chapter. Research that identifies successful strategies for maintaining an athlete's focus reinforces the importance of goal setting.

Here, understanding the different types of goals that exist is important:

- Outcome goals are about winning and losing and often involve a variety of factors outside of the athlete's control.
- Performance goals are focused on tasks relevant to the athlete's performance and are, therefore, within the athlete's control.

As one might imagine, research proves that athletes who focus on performance goals like increasing the first-pitch strike percentage or playing longer periods of foul-free basketball achieve greater focus. Athletes who focus on outcome goals like striking out more batters or winning the game are less likely to achieve focus-related success.

The increased concentration ability for athletes who focus on performance goals is likely to result from fewer external distractions. In the above example, the pitcher who focuses on the performance goal of throwing more first-pitch strikes is concentrating solely on their controllable task-relevant performance. In contrast, a pitcher who focuses on the outcome goal of striking out more batters is likely to be distracted by external variables like the batter's statistics, place in the batting order or performance of their last bat.

Positive Self-Talk

To maintain focus as they train and compete, many athletes talk to themselves.

Yes, they talk to themselves.

They remind themselves, silently, about their ability, their preparedness, certain skills they want to employ, etc. Others talk to themselves less positively.

How athletes talk to themselves is so important.

The problem is that for human beings, the default setting is to rely upon habitual vocabulary or the vocabulary that exists beneath our consciousness. When athletes experience stress or other negative emotions, they have the human tendency to draw from that habitual vocabulary. For many people, the habitual vocabulary can be quite negative.

The words we think and speak become our experience. Words have a biochemical effect on the body. For example, when an athlete uses a phrase like "we got crushed" in a negative way, they will produce very different biochemical effects than if they were to say, "We lost, but we know what to work on."

Human beings have needs that must be met. Athletes have those same needs. One need is to feel safe and supported. The inner voice of an athlete has more power than many realize.

We use words to interact with others daily, but the words we choose to speak and think can have a significant impact on how we feel, behave, train, and perform.

Try this:

- Change just one keyword in your vocabulary by removing a negative one or including a new word that inspires you.
- Aim to use this new word once a day verbally, once a day in your journal, and many times a day in your thoughts about the training and competing.

Through this simple activity, athletes can begin to change their routine vocabulary and self-talk habits to change how they think, feel, and perform drastically.

Transforming your vocabulary accesses the power to change your experiences by lowering the intensity and impact of negative emotions and turning up the volume of positive emotions and experiences, almost like the dial on a stereo.

Trigger Words

Some athletes use a type of code called trigger words. Trigger words are words or phrases that trigger certain reminders or emotions in the athlete. Athletes have used trigger words for decades.

Marathon runners count steps using the numbers as trigger words to maintain concentration.

Gymnasts might tell themselves to 'push' on the vault.

Basketball players or runners on the basepath in a baseball game might use trigger words like "be aggressive."

Golfers often select trigger phrases that result in desired body posture. For example, when taking a shot with a nine iron, a trigger phrase like "cut the grass" forces the player to keep his or her head down on the ball rather than a phrase like "follow-through" which would be more likely to draw the player's head up.

When Serena Williams defeated her sister Venus in 2002 at Wimbledon, she pulled out handwritten notes in between games. She told reporters after the match she had written notes for herself with the trigger words "stay low" and "hit in front."

To maximize efficacy, trigger words and phrases should be brief and worded in a positive way that encourages the pursuit, rather than the avoidance, of a particular behavior. Athletes should experiment during training with words that:

- Provide vivid imagery of success
- Instill confidence
- Drive concentration

POINTS TO REMEMBER

- To achieve flow during a competition,

athletes must do everything in their power to put themselves on 'autopilot' by trusting their practice and training to take over.
- When a mistake is made in competition, it is critically important to let it go immediately.
- Athletes should examine their performance to identify the most common situations where they encounter difficulty and practice working through such situations during training exercises.
- Research suggests that an athlete's recall of information is facilitated by conditions that look, sound, and feel like those where the original training took place.
- Because athletics are heavily ritualized, successful athletes have realized that consistently engaging in preparatory rituals promote excellent performance. Consistent and repetitive training can't happen without motivation.
- Being able to focus is one thing. Focusing in the right way and on the right things is another.

CHAPTER THREE

VISUALIZATION AND MENTAL TRAINING

WHAT IS VISUALIZATION?

TRY THIS:

Go to a quiet place.

Focus your attention on your breath. As you inhale, follow your breath and imagine seeing it as it moves through your body, through your lungs, and back out through your exhalation.

Release any tension in your face and shoulders as you take each breath. With each breath, relax a little more.

Now, close your eyes as you continue breathing and focus on your breath until you are fully relaxed.

Open your eyes and continue this exercise.

Imagine yourself arriving at a competition, game, or match.

Where are you?

Who are you competing against?

What do you see?
What do you hear?
What do you feel?
What do you smell?

Now, see yourself performing at your very best. Perhaps at a level, you have not yet achieved. Be specific. See each skill being executed at the very best of your ability and maybe even beyond your current ability.

Close your eyes, continue to breathe slowly and deeply, and spend a good amount of time creating the experience from start to end. Once the experience is over, return to the breathing exercise and let the experience settle in your mind and throughout your body.

When you're ready, open your eyes.

Consider these questions. You might even want to write down your answers in a sports journal, which we will discuss later.

When you saw yourself performing, what did you see?

What was your physical posture like?

When you executed certain skills, how did that look?

What sounds were reassuring? What sounds were distracting or even threatening?

Examine the experience and review what you noticed.

This Is the Process of Visualization.

The process will be different for every athlete depending on the sport, the level of experience, the skills under construction, etc. However, the concept is generally the same across the board.

When athletes visualize, they purposefully and intentionally rehearse a skill, a routine, or a play in their mind's eye to feel the process of creating a successful outcome.

Whether you realize it or not, all athletes visualize in one way or another.

Our minds think using images. The way some athletes employ visualization can improve performance. In contrast, other athletes who unintentionally visualize improperly can cause damage to their performance.

An athlete who unknowingly replays their mistakes or missed opportunities repeatedly will only hurt their performance in the long run.

However, when athletes employ properly guided and intentional visualization, great results can be achieved.

WHY SHOULD WE VISUALIZE?

Mental imagery enables the athlete's mind to simulate a perfectly executed routine, throw to first, three-point shot, or shot on goal.

A gymnast will see herself executing the perfect gymnastics routine and feel herself nailing a steady landing. This process is used by many athletes to rehearse for competition cognitively.

It's more than just seeing the goal ahead of you. When athletes go into the future and live there in vivid detail for a bit, they can define their reality and essentially create a blueprint for what is possible.

When athletes visualize, they tap into the part of the

brain that is later going to perform the actual physical activity.

Jordan Spieth

Some say that golfer Jordan Spieth won the Masters using visualization.

Spieth's coach since the age of 12, Cameron McCormick, has always been fascinated by how the brain works for elite athletes and considers himself a lifelong student of the mental game.

McCormick encouraged Spieth to visualize his shots and watch the shots of others and visualize those too. McCormick understood how activating what is known as mirror neurons would enable Spieth to mimic later the movement that would produce the desired results.

As athletes work to improve any skill - for Spieth, it is the golf swing - they create new neural pathways that trigger muscle memory. By activating these mirror neurons, athletes essentially learn in their minds before they learn with their bodies. Those mirror neurons can also be reactivated as you compete simply by watching your competitors or by visualizing yourself nailing that perfect shot.

Many coaches have followed McCormick's lead and now have their players write down their most memorable shots in golf or basketball, hits in baseball, or serves in tennis, and practice recalling them so the athlete can recreate these experiences in their minds and later with their bodies.

Spieth is known for visualizing and being incredibly fixated on his target. He can see a tiny branch on a tree to aim for. He'll then picture the trajectory of the ball and what shape it will take. He'll even see how the ball reacts when it lands.

Every one of these steps helps his body move in the right way to produce the desired outcome.

Research proves that practicing mental visualization improves skill learning and performance during competition.

Visualization stimulates the same regions of the brain that are activated during any physical exertion or completion—accordingly, visualization conditions the brain to automatically expect and operate at levels that produce successful outcomes. The more often an athlete's mind has rehearsed the optimal performance, the more ingrained the successful habits will become.

Professional athletes and their coaching staff give so much weight to visualization that it is not uncommon for teams to dedicate entire practice sessions to mental pregame walk-through.

WHAT ARE THE BENEFITS?

All teams, from baseball to hockey, can employ visualization to rehearse or walk-through the desired skill execution the day before an important competition to reinforce skills and strategies.

Performance

Research proves that the mental activities athletes use to prepare themselves are just as important as the physical elements. Even your muscles benefit from visualization.

The brain can interpret visualization strategies in the same way it interprets the actual physical act. When athletes see themselves becoming stronger, faster, and more skilled, the mind helps the body make it happen.

Expectations

When athletes visualize themselves performing well in a competition and live that moment repeatedly, they tend to envision what might go wrong and what challenges to expect. By having the chance to think about ways to solve those problems in advance, the athlete can eliminate some unknown variables that can contribute to anxiety. The mind is then prepared to react to whatever comes its way. When you expect the unexpected, you have a better chance at controlling what might otherwise be an uncontrollable situation.

Confidence

Athletes can benefit from a boost in confidence through visualization. When you see yourself living your best performance, you are more likely to believe it is possible. Whether it's throwing that first-pitch strike, nailing that perfect landing, or defending the leading scorer like a beast, visualization allows you to see it and believe it.

Research proves that simply visualizing yourself receiving praise from a coach or teammates results in improved self-esteem.

Motivation

Visualization enables athletes to sustain motivation. Seeing your best self-accomplishing athletic performance provides an organic dose of inspiration. What you focus on becomes larger in your mind. Therefore, not only focusing on positive skill execution, positive results, and the desired outcome but seeing it and feeling it increases the likelihood of it happening. It's a natural producer of motivation that can get you through a particularly difficult workout or situation in competition.

WHICH TOP ATHLETES ARE VISUALIZING AND WHAT HAVE THEY ACCOMPLISHED?

Athletes also use visualization and mental imagery to improve their ability to focus.

Michael Phelps

Let's talk about Michael Phelps. His habits have earned him the most Olympic gold medals of any athlete in history. One of those habits is mental imagery.

Phelps uses mental imagery to visualize and feel

every stroke and turn within each race. His coach, Bob Bowman, required Phelps to run a mental video each morning and every night before turning in. Bowman wanted Phelps to see, feel, and hear every aspect of the race from how the starting block would feel on his feet to the sights and sounds of celebration after winning the race. Bowman would encourage Phelps to "play the tape" during training sessions.

Bowman said that this process enabled Phelps to "concentrate on these tiny moments of success and build them into mental triggers... It's more like his habits had taken over. The actual race was just another step in a pattern that started earlier that day and was nothing but victories. Winning became a natural extension" (Cohn, n.d.).

Lindsey Vonn

One of the greatest skiers in U.S, history, Olympic gold medalist Lindsey Vonn uses visualization in a very modern way.

Vonn, who began skiing at just three years old, loves using technology to advance her performance. She uses fitness trackers like the rest of us. Still, she wears wearable cameras to record performance from her point of view for later assessment purposes.

The technology that she finds the most useful is virtual reality. Its power is to take visualization to the next level.

Vonn feels visualization gives her a competitive edge because not every athlete taps into its limitless power.

"If everyone were given that opportunity to train -- to virtually train all the courses -- then it wouldn't be an advantage for me," she says with a laugh. "So I prefer if they wait a couple of years on that" (Guglielmo, 2015).

Vonn says that one thing she is good at is visualizing the course in her mind.

By the time she gets to the start gate, she has mentally run the race a hundred times, picturing exactly how she'll take each turn.

Once she visualizes the course, she never forgets it.

Vonn doesn't stop there, however. She is known to physically simulate the moves she plans to make by shifting her body in the way she plans to do it on the course. She even practices her breathing routine for competition as she is visualizing.

When there is no snow and no skiing, visualization allows Vonn to maintain all of this mental training still.

Arnold Schwarzenegger

Schwarzenegger is a bodybuilder who has always used visualization to reach his goals. For him, visualization is creating a vision of the athlete you want to become and then living and behaving as if you are already there.

"I had this fixed idea of growing a body like Reg Park's. The model was there in my mind; I only had to grow enough to fill it," he explained. "The more I focused in on this image and worked and grew, the more I saw it was real and possible for me to be like him" (Williams, n.d.).

Jack Nicklaus

Jack Nicklaus is a champion in a sport where visualization is big.

The golfer swears he has never swung the club, not even when practicing, without visualizing a focused image of what that swing will look like.

"First I see the ball where I want it to finish, nice and white and sitting up high on the bright green grass. Then the scene quickly changes, and I see the ball going there; its path, trajectory, and shape, even its behavior on landing" (Clarey, 2014).

Emily Cook

This aerial skier, two time Olympian, and five-time national champion shared how visualization impacted her team's experience at the 2014 Sochi Olympics.

At the starting gate, her entire team was visualizing as they prepared themselves to compete. "We're all up there, flapping our arms," Cook said. "It looks insane, but it works" (Clarey, 2014).

Although Winter Olympics are events where the environment is relatively controlled, Cook's sport of aerial skiing, where jump sequences can last up to 10 seconds, involves wind or weather patterns that can vary.

She and her team create imagery scripts and use

scripted audio recordings to break down every element and every step to arrive at the exact jump she wanted to execute.

"I would say into the recorder: 'I'm standing on the top of the hill. I can feel the wind on the back of my neck. I can hear the crowd,'" Cook said. "Kind of going through all those different senses and then actually going through what I wanted to do for the perfect jump. I turn down the in-run. I stand up. I engage my core. I look at the top of the jump" (Clarey, 2014).

Cook plays the recording back for herself with eyes closed. She relaxes and feels each movement in her muscles. This mental work, she says, helped her become a better athlete.

Cook has used visualization for more than just competition.

She uses it to break negative thought patterns when she experiences them. The practice enables her to switch from negative to positive thoughts when at the starting gate.

She has also used visualization for healing purposes. When she suffered an injury that sidelined her for over two years, she and one of the U.S. team's nine sports psychologists at the Sochi Olympics, Nicole Detling, used visualization to see and feel her bones healing.

Billie Jean King

More than 40 years ago, Billie Jean King, winner of 20 Wimbledon titles, knew the power of visualization.

The tennis champion led the revolution for underpaid female players. It gained global notoriety during the 1973 exhibition match with Bobby Riggs, a notoriously self-proclaimed male chauvinist.

King used visualization to imagine anything that could go wrong and see herself reacting in an ideal manner. Whether it was the weather, a line call, or a delay, she tried to find examples of situations that would be out of her control and mentally see herself working through the problem.

"I would think about how I wanted to act. Like they teach in acting, 'act as if ...' — it's the same thing in sports. Do you stand up straight? Do you have your body language speaking confidently? Because 75% of the time when you're on the court, you're not hitting a ball. And I think that's where the champions come through. So I would visualize all these different possibilities" (*Pioneer Billie Jean King moved the baseline for women's tennis*, 2014).

She would advise those she mentored to visualize themselves swinging the racket and hitting 50 forehand shots and 50 backhand shots in a row.

As she played, she focused on specific goals like returning serves to a particular spot on the court. In her visualization strategies, King always emphasized the importance of focusing on her performance on her side of the net. She visualized herself standing up straight, staying in the present moment, and immediately letting go of mistakes to remain present.

MENTAL TRAINING

Earlier in this chapter, we touched upon the idea that everything we do is motivated by the desire to avoid pain or achieve pleasure. We also noted that the brain operates on associations rather than logic.

Let's now use this information and program the brain with associations.

Do you want to avoid a particular behavior? Teach the brain to associate it with pain.

If you'd like to stop staying up so late, associate late bedtime with pain—journal about the cost to you when you stay up late.

- Do you sleep later and miss a morning run?
- Do you find yourself feeling sluggish the next day and giving weaker effort during practice or workouts?
- Is your attitude more negative?
- What else are you missing out on by sleeping late?
- What other pain is being generated in your life?
- What does it cost?
- What else could you accomplish if you were up earlier and had more energy?
- How does it make you feel that you watched television instead of doing an activity that would make you feel productive?
- Calculate the number of hours of life you've

missed out on by sleeping late.

Focus on all of the downsides of this behavior. Reread it later and add to it. The more you focus on the negative sides of the unwanted behavior and the more intense the feeling is, the sooner your brain will create an association between pain and staying up late.

The same is right about teaching the brain to associate pleasure with behaviors you want to nurture and experience more consistently.

Imagine you are a runner just starting. You always run two and a half miles. You know you can run three miles, but you never do. Journal about what running that extra half mile would be like.

- How accomplished would you feel?
- How motivated would you feel?
- How would your life be better if you increase your endurance?
- What athletic goals would become easier to achieve with this added endurance?
- Imagine yourself walking and cooling down at a different endpoint on your run with a confident smile.

Again, read the entry later and add to it. The more you focus on all the positive effects of this desired behavior, the sooner your brain will create an association between pleasure and running that extra distance.

Have fun with these exercises. Free yourself from

your old beliefs and remember that your brain can be trained to remove limitations.

HOW CAN ATHLETES PRACTICE MENTAL REHEARSAL?

When athletes arrive at the elite levels, every player there has the physical ability necessary to compete. What sets apart the athletes who will find real success is mental toughness.

Being able to master your thoughts and emotions after making a mistake and moving forward with confidence and composure is where the real power lies.

Mental training is a branch of sports psychology that focuses on helping athletes break through psychological barriers that prevent them from achieving peak performance.

Too many athletes and coaches resist or entirely disregard mental training because they don't understand it and therefore, can't see all of its benefits.

For athletes to optimize their performance and achieve their personal best, understanding mental training's value is critical.

Mental training will benefit the athlete by:

- Improving attitude and mental skills by identifying limiting beliefs
- Embracing healthy philosophies about their performance and their sport
- Addressing mental barriers like unrealistic

expectations, fear of failure, and perfection
- Enhancing confidence and focus
- Building trust with coaches and trainers

Just like physical skills, mental skills require planning, commitment, repetition, and game-time application to be successful.

Begin With the End In Mind

You've likely heard that great planning begins with the end in mind. Almost like programming your GPS, you tell your brain this is where you want to go, and it will get you there. It's the same for athletics.

While planning for challenging situations is useful, and we will cite that as an important step, it's critical to begin the practice of visualization for athletic performance with the optimal outcome in mind.

See, feel, and hear your ideal athletic performance from start to end. During this step, train your mind to focus on only positive images. If you begin to play negative outcomes, be patient with yourself.

When practicing meditation, try to focus on your breathing and nothing else. If an unwanted thought enters your mind, calmly acknowledge it and send it on its way. Refocus yourself and begin again.

Call Upon Your Senses

See in vivid color. Whether you visualize the white

strip down the basepath or the still water before your dive pierces it, see every aspect of your performance. Smell the victory. Smell the chalk in the gym, the smell of a newly opened can of tennis balls, or the chlorine of the pool as you visualize.

Hear the sounds, whether they are the positive cheering of the crowd or the negative calls from the opposing team's fans. Prepare yourself mentally to deal with anything that comes your way.

Feel the bat in your hands or the exhilaration of completing your longest or fastest run.

Internal and External Imagery

In the exercise at the beginning of the chapter, were you watching yourself as if in a video, essentially seeing your entire body as others would? Or were you seeing through your own eyes and from your perspective?

Maybe you alternated back and forth between these two perspectives.

Athletes can benefit from using internal imagery, sometimes called associated visualization, that leverages visualizing the experience through their own eyes and from their point of view. Athletes will find that this method enables a deep connection to the feelings involved during the visualization, critically important to the success of this strategy.

They should also explore external imagery, sometimes called disassociated visualization, where the athlete sees themselves from a third-person point of view or as if watching themselves on video. Benefits from this method can be found when athletes work through an event that was particularly difficult, deflating, or painful to gain perspective and wisdom. It can also help you achieving something outside of your current ability level.

Athletes can and should experiment to determine which method works best and the ideal combination of imagery methods for their particular needs. At different points in their athletic careers, the combination might change, so frequent reassessment is beneficial. Adapting the practice of visualization to align with new goals means you are using visualization effectively. It's an effective practice that all athletes should adopt.

Practice Visualization Consistently

If visualizing is not a regular practice in your athletic arsenal, you've probably tried meditating or visualizing only to find yourself daydreaming a few minutes in. That is a normal occurrence. Minds wander. Period.

Athletes who give up on visualization techniques are usually those that have not practiced enough or consistently enough.

The good news is every athlete can visualize effectively.

Visualization, just like meditation, is a mental muscle that becomes stronger when flexed and practiced. Treat this element of your mental training just as important as physical training. Schedule it into your everyday warm-up routine.

Visualize In a Relaxed State

Because athletes are typically under pressure when in competition, it's important to recall visualization techniques during stressful moments.

However, whenever possible, practicing visualization in a relaxed environment is most beneficial.

Call Upon Trigger Words

We discussed trigger words in our chapter about consistency and focus. Trigger words can also be very effective as an athlete employs visualization.

Some athletes imagine a red balloon filled with stress. The trigger word 'pop' helps them visualize a pin piercing the balloon and the stress slipping away. The athlete can remind themselves that using the trigger word or phrase can be used by the coach when necessary.

When trigger words are practiced in conjunction with visualization, it will be easy for the athlete to recall strategies that have been practiced.

Use Imagery Journals

Imagery journals can be used in a few ways.

Writing down the skills and execution specifics that an athlete desires can help maintain consistent visualization.

Logging how effectively the imagery is producing

results is also helpful. For example, if a trigger word worked well in a game, recording the details will help solidify the concept in your mind.

Mental Toughness

Imagine a job where every time you make a mistake or something gets by you, a red siren blares, and the entire stadium stands up and screams. That's the life of a hockey goalie.

NHL goalie Matt O'Connor knows all about this. In his college days at Boston University (BU), his team made it to the Hockey East championship. A harmless shot by an opponent that he had routinely caught a million times slipped from his glove and fell between his legs. As he tried to retrieve it, he inadvertently knocked it into the goal. BU lost that game, and its hope for a championship was over.

So how did O'Connor recover from that devastating loss and go on to play in the NHL?

Mental toughness.

"Everybody gets scored upon," says Miller. "Maybe not quite as dramatically, or in the theater that this was, but everyone gets scored on. As a goalie, you have to learn how to let it go and get back to the present. The mantra is, 'Next shot. See it, and stop it.' That's all the goalie should be thinking" (O'Connor, 2015).

Mental toughness is about controlling the mind game. How athletes talk to themselves, maintain their composure, and eliminate distractions is critical.

Athletes must teach themselves a process that has no tolerance for a negative judgment. It's training yourself to move on to the next thing and seeing mistakes as part of the bigger picture that includes all of the times the athlete has executed positively.

After that championship game, O'Connor had to face reporters and answer questions about the mistake. This was an important first step in the test of his mental toughness. Understanding that being vulnerable and making mistakes is part of the athletic process strengthens the player as an athlete and as a human being.

POINTS TO REMEMBER

- When athletes visualize, they purposefully and intentionally rehearse a skill, a routine, or a play in their mind's eye in order and feel the process of creating a successful outcome.
- Research proves that the mental activities athletes use to prepare themselves are just as important as the physical elements. When athletes see themselves becoming stronger, faster, and more skilled, the mind helps the body make it happen.
- The brain operates on associations rather than logic.
- What sets apart the athletes who will find real success is mental toughness.

CHAPTER FOUR

SLEEP, REST, AND RECOVER

IF A TRAINER TOLD an athlete about a new strategy that reduces hormones in the body associated with stress, naturally increases human growth hormone, speeds up recovery time, and is proven to improve performance, what do you think that athlete would say?

The athlete would likely say, "Where do I sign up?"

Sleep is that strategy.

Sleep, rest, and recovery are essential for athletic performance and overall well-being.

This information is not new.

However, its effectiveness is a new concept for many athletes.

What is also new is the attention that researchers and coaches are beginning to pay to the importance of sleep, rest, and recovery play in athletic performance.

In many sports, games are often decided by the little things - inches, one missed shot, etc.

Athletes go to great lengths to get that winning edge. Since they were young, their families spent thousands of dollars on equipment, trainers, and expensive elite travel teams. Professional athletes spend thousands of dollars on offseason training regimens. They exhibit superhuman self-control, sometimes cutting out sugar or power loading protein. NFL players have even been known to have installed hyperbaric oxygen chambers to promote faster recovery from injuries.

Isn't it surprising then, that the free and easy resource of sleep - that can be the difference-maker in these games of inches - isn't placed higher on the priority list?

This chapter will examine why coaches must understand the physical and psychological benefits that rest and recovery after training and competition provide. It will also examine how psychological recovery depends on high-quality sleep and periods of wakeful rest.

WHAT TOOK SO LONG?

Although many professional athletes recognize the importance of rest for physical and mental well-being, coaches and trainers have been slow to guide optimal rest schedules and preventative and therapeutic strategies for achieving adequate sleep, rest, and recovery.

Research about best practices has produced very little useful information about rest. This is because the concept of rest, in general, has been overlooked when compared with sports psychology studies that focus on physical training and competition.

Explanations for this oversight include:

Rest is not exciting. The natural tendency is to focus on what is exciting. Let's face it. The inactivity associated with sleep, rest, and recovery is not as exciting as the physical actions required to execute the perfect play or to win the championship.

Stakeholders think they have no vested interest. The outcome of athletics (e.g., winning a competition or breaking a record) is important to all stakeholders. The seeming lack of correlation can cause it to be a low priority or not prioritized at all for stakeholders.

Out of sight, out of mind. Rest takes place behind the scenes, away from the training and competition site. It cannot be easy to value what cannot typically be observed and measured.

Rest is self-explanatory. To scientists and medical professionals who understand the intricate details of biology and cell repair, educating athletes about the benefits of rest and recovery might seem logical and worthwhile. Those who do not understand such things might consider rest to be too obvious, simple, and self-explanatory to include in an athlete's training program. When this happens, analysis of the concept falls off the radar.

Social lag has been largely ignored. A significant problem for collegiate and professional athletes has been swept under the rug for many years. Hangovers, or social lags as many call them, have a disruptive effect on sleep and, of course, on overall athletic performance. Believe it or not, alcohol use is widespread in the world of sports. Although many don't want to believe it or even acknowledge it, it is discussed a bit more openly as time goes on. However, research about the effects of alcohol on sleep and athletic performance is limited because of the sensitive nature of the topic and athletes' willingness to participate in such research.

Cultural norms generally undervalue rest. Society connects the dots between Type A personalities, overachievers, more work, and less sleep. The cultural and societal norms can subconsciously influence how people perceive the value of rest. Striving for goals, even unrealistic goals, tends to be highly valued in today's culture, and failure is thought to be something temporary, sometimes even self-imposed, that can be overcome by relentless hard work.

Athletic culture is often characterized by aggressive and competitive behavior, values results, and performance. Placing excessive importance on such dynamic values can cause athletes to feel lazy if they prioritize rest and recovery.

This last explanation has been particularly powerful in downplaying the benefits of rest and recovery. Research has found that athletes are often more motivated and disciplined when it comes to training than when putting forth effort toward healthy rest and sleep habits.

These researchers developed a strategy that labeled athletes who did not rest as lazy, since achieving adequate periods of rest and recovery time seemed to require more effort and self-discipline than the training itself.

Athletes will benefit from a better understanding of these reasons. That better understanding can lead to an enhanced concentration of efforts toward learning about the benefits upon recovery, motor skill learning, and performance of rest.

Athletes have likely experienced some of the following as a result of insufficient rest:

- Physical and psychological fatigue
- Mood swings
- Performance decline
- Burnout

With an increased focus on and understanding of incorrect perceptions surrounding recovery, athletes can adjust habits and improve performance and overall well-being.

WHY IS SLEEP IMPORTANT?

The correct quality and quantity of sleep protect mental health, physical health, quality of life, and safety.

When you sleep, your body works to keep your brain healthy and maintain physical well-being. It prepares the brain for the next day's activity. Sleep prepares the brain to form new pathways to support learning and remembering information.

For children and teens, sleep plays a significant role in physical, mental, and emotional growth.

Sleep is involved in the body's process of healing and repairing heart and blood vessels.

Sleep maintains hormonal balance. This is important for athletes because hormonal shifts can impact appetite, healthy nutrition, and energy.

Sleep also regulates how insulin impacts your body, your blood glucose levels, and energy.

The quality of sleep is important. Deep sleep triggers the release of a hormone that boosts muscle mass and helps cells and tissues repair themselves in children, teens, and adults.

An athlete's immune system relies on sleep to keep the body healthy.

Circadian Rhythm

Like breathing, the circadian rhythm is a pattern that is essential for the body. As in every other area of training, rhythm is important. The human body is designed to sync with rhythmic changes in the daily rhythms of light and dark changes.

In healthy athletes, physiological and biochemical variables such as body temperature, cortisol, melatonin, thyroid-stimulating hormone, noradrenaline, and serotonin show signs of the circadian rhythm. Disrupting circadian rhythm can decrease the production of natural testosterone and human growth hormone production.

Jet Lag and Social Lag

Daytime sleep can be a problem for athletes experiencing jet lag or social lag. Urges for daytime sleep results when you are tired. It's critically important for players to push through that urge and maintain active behavior. If enough hours are not spent active and out of bed during the day, the next night's sleep can also be interrupted. A negative pattern can easily emerge and interrupt well-established routines. Athletes should push through just as they would at practice and engage in physical activity outside in the natural light. Something as simple as walking can make the difference in getting sleep back on track.

Athletes must maintain a natural circadian rhythm. Jet lag and even the social lag from a late-night are part of life, and they are going to happen. If athletes properly plan for these types of interruptions, they can find their way back to circadian rhythm and regain the balance it provides.

In 2015, the New York Jets traveled to London to play the Miami Dolphins. The Jets were incredibly prepared. The fact that they packed their toilet paper was not the most interesting. They began preparing for the jet lag months in advance.

The Jets had to set the players' circadian rhythms five hours ahead, to Greenwich Mean Time. That's a tall order.

The general rule for overseas travel is that the body needs one day to adjust per time zone crossed. The Jets left New Jersey on a Thursday night. The game was going to be played Sunday afternoon in London. There were not enough days in between to adjust using the general rule.

Jim Maas, the retired Cornell professor who coined the term "power nap" a few decades ago and the sleep advisor for the Jets at the time, developed a plan.

The plan included rules that became increasingly important as the trip approached:

- "No caffeine after 2 p.m.
- No alcohol within three hours of bedtime.
- Keep room temperature between 65 and 68 degrees.
- Turn off or cover any blue, green or white lights in the bedroom, no matter how small.
- Nap for either 30 minutes, arising before you slip into deep sleep, or 90 minutes, after completing a sleep cycle, but never 60 minutes, because waking up in the middle of deep sleep can make you feel sluggish" (Mustard, 2015).

That was the simple stuff.

Each player arrived in his London hotel room and found a kit, purchased by the Jets for approximately $100, with orange-colored glasses. The glasses block the light from electronic devices that interfere with sleep. The players were instructed to wear orange glasses while using phones or studying film on tablets late at night.

Players also used Litebooks, iPhone-sized devices that claim to reset circadian rhythms by waking the body up in the new time zone with a beam of 10,000-lux white light.

The Dolphins also put stock in sleep, but not to the same degree as the Jets. In Miami, the Dolphins' training facility in 2015 had a sleeping room with electronic relaxation systems.

The Jets won that game in London 27-14. Whether it was because of the orange glasses, no one will ever really know. It's safe to say it didn't hurt.

HOW MUCH SLEEP DO ATHLETES NEED?

The athletic performance of professional and amateur athletes alike can benefit from more sleep. The more you train, the more sleep you require. And due to the additional physical stress that athletic training places on your muscles and nervous system, your body needs more time to recover.

The exact amount of required sleep will vary from athlete to athlete, but eight to ten hours are generally recommended.

Roger Federer and LeBron James have reportedly been known to sleep on average 12 hours per night. Federer even once said, "If I don't sleep 11 to 12 hours per day, it's not right" (National Sleep Foundation, 2020).

What the Experts Say

According to the American Academy of Sleep Medicine:

- Adults require between seven and nine hours of sleep to optimize performance and health.
- Adolescents require additional sleep, ideally between eight and 10 hours.
- It has been suggested that athletes require nine to 10 hours of sleep to promote recovery between workouts.

The ideal amount of sleep will vary among different individuals depending on recent sleep history, age, exertion levels, illness, and stress factors.

Quantity vs. Quality

Quantity, or duration, is only one way to assess sleep. Sleep quality is also critical.

Recent guidance from the National Sleep Foundation indicates that sleep quality improves for athletes of all ages when sleep continuity is achieved. Sleep continuity is defined as routine bedtime and decreased nighttime awakenings.

HOW DOES SLEEP DEPRIVATION AFFECT PERFORMANCE?

The right quantity and quality of sleep at the right times can help athletes function at optimal levels.

However, athletes who are sleep deprived are less productive, have slower reaction times, make more mistakes, and put themselves in real danger.

Several nights of sleep loss — even as little as one to two hours per night — deteriorates a person's ability to function to the same degree as if they hadn't slept at all for a day or even two.

Lack of sleep can cause microsleep or brief moments of sleep that occur while awake.

If you have ever driven to practice and not remembered part of the drive, you may have experienced microsleep. Just as scary as driving while experiencing microsleep is practicing or playing a contact sport while experiencing microsleep. Athletes can miss critical information and put themselves in real danger.

Some athletes do not know at all about the risks associated with sleep deficiency. Many do not even know that they are sleep deficient.

Being sleep deficient can cause harm in an instant. An athlete can be distracted during a play or react slower than normal and sustain a devastating injury.

Sleep deficiency can also harm athletes over time. Making decisions, solving problems, and coping with change can become more difficult over time. Chronic health problems can also result from a persistent lack of sleep.

Children and teen athletes who are sleep deficient can experience problems getting along with others, which can impact the team dynamic. Tired athletes are more likely to experience more stress, feel angry, behave impulsively, and lack motivation. They also may have problems paying attention in class, get lower grades, and have trouble maintaining eligibility.

Sleep deficiency has also been linked to depression and risk-taking behavior, neither of which are positive factors for athletes.

A PROPER NIGHT'S SLEEP DOES A BODY GOOD

Researchers tracked the Stanford University basketball team for several months. The players added an average of two hours to their sleep totals each night. Here is what they learned:

- Players increased their speed by 5%
- Free throws were 9% more accurate
- Reflexes were firing faster
- Player felt happier

Other studies show similar benefits for football players and athletes involved in many other sports.

Another study of adult athletes included sleep journals before, and during, a national tournament to evaluate the relationship between sleep and competitive success. The two teams with the best performance and resulting highest placement in the tournament reported significantly more quality sleep duration.

Endurance Performance and Anaerobic Power

When compared to athletes who were sleep-deprived, well-rested athletes were able to achieve:

- Greater distance covered on a 30-minute self-paced treadmill test
- Increased time to exhaustion
- Improved rates of recovery between bouts of strenuous exercise
- More desirable pre-exercise muscle glycogen stores that may translate to improved endurance efforts

Accuracy and Reaction Time

When compared to athletes who were sleep-deprived, well-rested athletes were able to achieve:

- Better accuracy in tennis serving, basketball free throws, and three-point field goals
- Improved reaction times

Learning and Executive Function

The ability and capacity for learning are critical for athletic development, progress, and performance. Sleep is critical for learning, memory, and overall cognitive processing.

In the earliest cycles of sleep, blood flow to muscles increases, and the human growth hormone is naturally released. This enables the body to grow and cells to repair. New information or skills learned in practice that day, like strategies in film study, are organized and reviewed in their mind. As the athlete continues to sleep, the brain integrates those new skills and strategies with existing knowledge. The final 'lap' of sleep is characterized by bursts of brain activity that create new muscle memories from that day's activities.

It seems like a lot to miss out on by skimping on sleep.

These particular benefits of sleep extension are particularly crucial for children, teens, and collegiate athletes. They must satisfy athletic demands in conjunction with academic requirements.

When compared to sleep-deprived athletes, well-rested athletes were able to achieve:

- Improved neurocognitive performance, i.e., quicker decision making
- Completion of sports-specific tasks with greater ease
- Outcomes that required flexible thinking
- Better self-control and decision making
- Improved mood and decreased fatigue, soreness, depression, and confusion

SLEEP TIPS

Athletes tend to overestimate the amount of sleep they get. One way to ensure an adequate amount of sleep is to plan. Strategize just as you would for a workout. Setting routines and establishing boundaries as outlined in the following tips will go a long way in ensuring that athletes get the amount of sleep they need.

Off Days

Dealing with sleep on your off days isn't as easy as it sounds. A day spent in bed doesn't necessarily add up to a well-rested athlete.

Winding down from a practice or a game is not easy. Athletes know they need rest, but not all rest and recovery strategies are equal. Managing downtime is just as important as managing schedules for training and competition if an athlete wants to optimize performance.

Collegiate and professional athletes might be tempted to celebrate and enjoy their celebrity status on days off. However, when it's time to get back to work, designing a plan for enjoying yourself, although it might sound crazy, is the way to go. How an athlete deals with their downtime is what separates the good from the great when it's time to train and compete again.

Acknowledging social lag, preparing for it, and knowing how to recover can mitigate performance disruptions without being a major buzzkill.

What the Pros Do

If you are skeptical about putting forth the effort to rest properly, think about these NFL teams and the lengths to which they have gone to prioritize sleep for their players.

- The Miami Dolphins and the New England Patriots have added dark rooms to their practice facilities to take naps.
- The Philadelphia Eagles players complete a morning questionnaire on their tablets, self-reporting how long they slept the previous night.
- When linebacker Demario Davis arrives at the Jets headquarters at 6 a.m. to study film, he studies in the glow of a team-issued Litebook. This space-age device maintains circadian rhythm by promoting alertness with a beam of white light with the same intensity as natural sunlight.

Everyday Tips

Athletes can take action to improve sleep habits. To improve sleep habits, athletes should:

- Go to bed and wake up at the same time every day. Maintain a consistent sleep schedule on weeknights and weekends.
- Integrate early morning and afternoon exercise to help maintain or even reset a healthy sleep-wake cycle by raising body temperature early enough in the day and allowing it to drop and trigger sleepiness later gradually.

- Use the hour before bed for quiet time. To the extent possible, adjust training schedules to avoid strenuous exercise at night.
- Avoid large meals before bedtime.
- Remember that the effects of caffeine can last as long as eight hours. A cup of tea or coffee at 2 p.m. can be a bad idea.
- Keep your bedroom quiet, cool, and dark. Eyeshades or blackout curtains can help.
- Consider a relaxation routine like meditation or a shower before bed to signal to your brain that it's time to wind down.
- Journal or list-write any concerns about upcoming training or competition events to help clear your mind before turning in.
- Keep a separate sleep diary to record behavior and sleep success outcomes. This can help identify patterns on nights where your sleep was ideal so you can replicate those patterns, and nights where you had difficulty so you can avoid those patterns.
- Limit naps. Take them earlier in the afternoon and for no more than 20 minutes.

Some athletes who struggle with achieving the proper rest are choosing to monitor their sleep patterns and carefully make changes in their diet, routines, and other habits. Athletes know that what can be measured can be managed. There are many strategies and even sleep tracking devices that can help. Athletes with persistent complaints of poor sleep or excessive daytime fatigue should consider additional measures, including:

- Screening for preexisting medical conditions such as insomnia, sleep-disordered breathing, restless legs syndrome, depression, anxiety, or concomitant illness.
- Adjusting training, sleep, and wake times before traveling to other time zones to incrementally 'practice' sleeping in the time zone of the destination. This is done to potentially shorten the required amount of sleep adjustment time upon arrival.

Athletes who prioritize regularly scheduled and well-structured rest time, even on their days off, can maintain and also improve performance without damaging their social lives. Consistent monitoring and measuring is the only way to manage sleep, rest, and recovery, and it is the key to gaining that competitive edge over competitors who don't prioritize these important elements of their craft.

POINTS TO REMEMBER

- Coaches must understand the physical and psychological benefits that rest and recovery after training and competition provide.
- With an increased focus on and

understanding of incorrect perceptions surrounding recovery, athletes can adjust habits and improve performance and overall well-being.
- Athletes know that what can be measured can be managed.

CHAPTER FIVE

HEALTHY EATING TO FUEL YOUR BODY

PHYSICS AND NUTRITION are not often discussed together, but perhaps they should be?

Newton's laws of motion tell athletes that objects remain at rest, or in the same patterns unless they are compelled to change their state by external actions or elements.

The external element, in this case, is nutrition. When athletes see nutrition as a force that can change their state, they may begin to place more weight on its importance.

However, nutrition books can be complicated and time-consuming. Often they are too scientific to be practical or helpful. Professional athletes rely on science and have teams of experts doing all of that dirty work for them. They also rely on common-sense practices that work.

The value of food for athletes should never be judged

by how much attention it is getting in pop culture. Nutrition should be the logical application of what athletes know about themselves and the primary scientific benefits of food.

See what different athletes are doing to enable nutrition—this external element—to impact the pattern within their actions and emotions.

Athletes understand that the physiology of athletic performance is not just based on energy production. An athlete's success requires proper nutrition for growth and continued development of muscles, mental function, and the immune system to fuel that energy production.

Professional athletes work with nutrition experts whose knowledge of the power behind the relations between carbs, fat, and protein has exponentially increased in the past few years and continues to do so every day. These experts advise athletes and develop personalized plans to consume balanced diets, hydrate properly, and tap into micronutrients from various foods to maximize performance.

This chapter will explore what professional athletes are learning from their nutritional advisors and will allow you to choose which plan makes the most sense.

WHY IS IT IMPORTANT TO FUEL YOUR BODY?

The body burns energy during daily activity and exercise. Food and liquids replenish the body's energy. Energy balance happens when you exert the same amount of energy as you consume. Sounds simple, right?

For athletes and especially those still in adolescence, a variety of other factors must be considered.

Increased nutritional needs

As an athlete's body mass grows, it requires more calories to maintain that energy. More intense workouts burn more calories, but athletes don't always compensate by increasing their caloric intake to account for the additional activity.

Nutritional information is lacking or misinformed

Athletes and parents often lack specific nutritional knowledge. It can be difficult without expert guidance to separate valid information from incorrect information.

Overscheduling interferes with meal planning

After practice, it's all too easy for athletes to grab a quick burger or skip dinner altogether. Planning amidst a busy schedule is critical if athletes consume an adequate number of calories from nutritional sources.

Fad or sustainability-conscious diets

Athletes who choose to become vegan, vegetarian, or gluten-free, among other dietary programs, might not appropriately plan for making up for lost calories and nutrients that are essential for the increased activity level in an athletic lifestyle such as calcium, protein, iron, or vitamin B-12.

Body image

Athletes are not immune to distorted thoughts about body image. The impacts upon diet and calorie restriction must be carefully considered and monitored to avoid serious nutritional deficiencies. Clinical eating disorders like bulimia and anorexia are certainly severe issues. The most prevalent problem common among athletes is consuming too few calories or calories that are not nutrient-dense enough to support rigorous athletic routines and performance.

Digestion

Whether you're an amateur runner, working out to lose some weight, or you are in the middle of a grueling season, intense workouts can impact your digestive system and put stress on your immune system. It's essential to pay attention to how you fuel your body and find the right combination of carbohydrates, protein, fat, vitamins, minerals, and fluids to maintain healthy digestion.

TOM BRADY

The TB12 Diet

The NFL legend has a new diet named after him called the TB12 Diet that is sometimes called the Tom Brady Diet.

The diet is largely composed of whole foods, and Brady attributes it to his football longevity. The diet has been said to lower the risk of injury, improve athletic performance, and drive recovery rates and energy levels.

The diet, which is not based on scientific facts, has been criticized for its unnecessary complexity. Critics also claim it is unsustainable in the long term.

Brady wrote a book in 2017 called the TB12 method that details 12 principles he uses for sustained athletic performance and excellence.

Like other diets, TB12 emphasizes eating whole foods that have been minimally processed and recommends avoiding foods that are believed to be acidifying or inflammatory. The diet promotes a variety of TB12 meals, snacks, and proprietary supplements.

This method combines the principles of other diets like the alkaline diet and the Mediterranean diet by promoting organic, locally grown, seasonal, and minimally processed foods.

The Rules

The majority of recommended foods for this diet, 80% to be exact, should come from organically grown fruits, vegetables, whole grains, nuts, seeds, and legumes. The remaining portion of the diet comes from lean meats that should meet several criteria. Fish must be wild-caught, and meat must be not only organic, antibiotic-free, and hormone-free but also from grass-fed animals.

Those on this diet are encouraged to avoid anything that might be acidifying or cause inflammation. Among those restricted items are dairy, most oils, foods containing soy and gluten, as well as nightshade vegetables like potatoes, peppers, and eggplant. As you may have guessed, food containing sugars, artificial sweeteners, trans fats, caffeine, MSG, and iodized salt are also off-limits, as is alcohol.

As if all of these guidelines weren't enough, Brady's plan also restricts combining foods. For example, fruits should not be eaten with other foods. High-protein foods like meat or fish should not be eaten with food rich in carbohydrates like sweet potatoes. Water should be avoided during, before, and after meals. However, it is necessary to drink a significant amount during the day.

Sample Menu

If you're left wondering what an athlete would eat this way, here is a sample meal plan:

Breakfast: Homemade granola stirred into coconut yogurt.

Lunch: Hearty vegetable-chicken soup with kale and brown rice vermicelli.

Dinner: Wild salmon tacos on GMO-free corn tortilla wraps served with a side green salad.

ALY RAISMAN

Aly Raisman last competed in the Olympics in 2016. The gold medal gymnast has since become a vocal advocate for sexual assault survivors and a supporter of the body positivity movement.

Raisman knows what routines can do to the lifestyle of an athlete. Although her diet was much more structured in 2016, she still considers herself an athlete and maintains an athlete's diet. The athlete in her thinks about food in terms of what will keep her most energized for the activity ahead.

Keeping It Simple

These days, Raisman's diet is largely plant-based. She says she eats what makes her feel good. It's as simple as that.

Her day begins with a glass of celery juice. Then she'll typically have hot water with lemon. If she opts for coffee, she'll add soy milk as she finds even the slightest bit of protein makes a difference for her considering the plant-based diet.

The Menu

After meditation or another form of exercise, she'll take a break for a mid-morning snack, which might be a seedy bagel or a bagel with nuts, again keeping an eye on the protein. Another snacking option for Raisman is cauliflower rice with sliced avocado.

For lunch, Aly often opts for vegetable broths and soups like broccoli and spirulina soup. By making a big batch, she can save herself time and have it for days.

Afternoon snacks might be her homemade guacamole or a smoothie. Smoothies can be different every day. Her latest ingredient is ashwagandha powder. Aly usually combines mixed berries, hemp hearts, a little soy milk, and chia seeds to create a powerful, protein-packed beverage. The supplement has been said to provide multiple benefits, including lowering cortisol, soothing joint pain, boosting memory, lowering blood sugar, and building muscle. It's important to note that the supplement is not for everyone, however. Some studies report that it can cause miscarriage.

Dinner is usually a heavy plate of veggies, although Raisman might include fish. Her go-to dinner is a plate of oven-roasted potatoes with a side of greens, like cucumbers and brussel sprouts.

She doesn't deprive herself of dessert, although she does keep it healthy and plant-based. She treated herself with frozen bananas blended with soy milk and topped with dairy-free chocolate chips.

RASHAD JENNINGS

This former NFL running back who played for the New York Giants, the Oakland Raiders, and the Jacksonville Jaguars has a busy schedule and is often traveling, but he always prioritizes clean eating.

Jennings' diet is both gluten-free and dairy-free.

Gluten-Free Lifestyle

Gluten-free diets are becoming increasingly popular with athletes. As the research is mostly inconclusive, gluten-free popularity needs to be carefully reviewed, along with the effects of gluten-free diets on athletic performance.

A survey of 910 Australian athletes reported that 41% are following gluten-free diets or trying to reduce gluten intake by more than 50%. The diet is so popular because many athletes experience gastrointestinal issues and believe the symptoms are caused by gluten.

Half of the athletes who used a gluten-free diet in the study reported an improvement in gastrointestinal symptoms that were sometimes combined with additional symptoms like fatigue. However, a double-blind study (participants did not know which diet they were on) of 13 endurance cyclists revealed no differences in gastrointestinal symptoms or overall well-being.

Some nutritionists urge athletes, especially those with increased caloric requirements during endurance training, to consider that they might be exposing themselves to nutrient deficiencies by choosing a gluten-free diet.

The Science Experiment

The gluten-free lifestyle works for this 35-year-old athlete, who recently competed in Dancing with the Stars. Jennings places a great deal of importance on being aware of what you put into your body since it will directly impact the results you are trying to achieve.

You might be wondering how a professional athlete like Jennings does not eat bread.

In high school, Jennings says he was an overweight kid with asthma who was a fifth-string running back. A high school coach eventually talked to him about his weight.

The self-described 'dork' tried an experiment. He left a McDonald's hamburger, some cheese, milk, and bread on the counter for three days. Next to that, he placed a plate of chicken, lettuce, and an unpeeled banana. After three days, the hamburger, cheese, milk, and bread had become thick and hard, while the chicken, lettuce, and banana had only slightly - and naturally - deteriorated. He put two and two together and figured if that's what's happening outside his body, the same was likely to be happening within.

This informal science project caused Jennings to begin a quest for more information. He met with doctors and nutritionists to learn more about healthy eating and ultimately decided to stop eating gluten.

The rest is history: Jennings went on to play Division 1 football in college before being drafted by the Jacksonville Jaguars in 2009. Now, he is an advocate for healthy eating, the Meatless Monday campaign, and works to spread the importance of nutrition through the Rashad Jennings Foundation.

The Menu

To achieve his personal best, Jennings plans out each meal with a personal chef and takes prepackaged meals on the road when his busy lifestyle has him traveling.

Jennings also incorporates a good deal of exercise into his routine, so his caloric intake exceeds 4,000 calories. Here is a sample meal plan he recently shared with Sports Illustrated:

Breakfast

Protein Shake: 2 scoops of Garden of Life vegan protein powder, ¼ cup organic rolled oats, 1 tbsp. organic raw flax seeds, one organic banana, 1 tbsp. organic peanut butter, 1 tbsp. organic coconut oil & 1 cup organic unsweetened almond milk.

Lunch

Turmeric chicken: 8 oz. organic free-range chicken

(with skin on), 1 cup sautéed vegetables (carrots, sweet peppers, green beans), ½ cup jasmine turmeric rice.

Herb grilled chicken baby green salad with organic cilantro lime avocado dressing: 3 oz. organic free-range boneless skinless chicken, 1.5 oz. organic baby greens, 3 oz. assorted raw veggies, 3 oz. organic cilantro lime avocado dressing.

Blueberries and almonds: 6 oz. organic raw blueberries, 3 oz. organic raw almonds.

Dinner

Coconut crusted salmon: 8 oz. wild-caught coho salmon, 1 cup steamed organic broccoli, 5 oz. roasted sweet potato.

Herb grilled chicken baby green salad with organic cilantro lime avocado dressing: 3 oz. organic free-range boneless skinless chicken, 1.5 oz. organic baby greens, 3 oz. assorted raw veggies, 3 oz. organic cilantro lime avocado dressing.

Apple and almonds: 1 organic gala apple, 3 oz. organic raw almonds.

Snacks

Organic coconut crusted chicken fingers: 4 oz. organic free-range boneless skinless chicken fingers and 2 oz. organic BBQ sauce.

KRISTIN ARMSTRONG

World-renowned professional cyclist Kristin Armstrong focuses on balance to properly fuel her body while actively training.

Carefully Planned Meals and Snacks

When preparing to fuel an athlete's body while in training mode, it is key to design and adhere to a plan. Many athletes unintentionally make poor choices when it comes to nutrition because they didn't plan.

With trophies, medals, and championships on the line, that seems silly.

Armstrong never skips breakfast and eats three daily balanced meals as well as a few nutritious snacks and doesn't eliminate any food groups. She maintains variety by mixing different carbohydrates, proteins, fruits, and vegetables into every meal and snack. She's lucky to have no food allergies, which allows her more freedom when designing her nutrition plan.

Keeping things simple is important. Armstrong is a mom and leads by example, so her family also thinks about fueling the body like an engine and seeing healthy foods as enablers for the body to make it operate stronger and faster.

Taking time to plan meals helps athletes manage cravings and avoid potential dietary pitfalls that result from impulsive decisions made by a hungry brain regarding food and drinks.

Breakfast Every Day

For many years, studies have focused on the importance of breakfast for good nutrition. Athletes especially require calories in the morning to fuel recovery and exercise. Breakfast boosts blood sugar, endurance, and performance.

Armstrong stresses the importance of breakfast in setting athletes up for success and shares that knowledge with her family.

Lots of Liquids

Athletes know they must remain hydrated, but proper hydration can be elusive when training is especially hard.

Even the slightest bit of dehydration can impact performance. Severe dehydration can be life-threatening.

For casual hydration throughout the day, Armstrong again keeps it simple with regular tap water and carbonated water with natural flavoring.

When drinking with meals or while on the bike things, she takes a different approach.

"I drink milk with my meals and make sure that when I am out training on my bike, my bottles are filled with a mix of water and electrolytes," she added. "Many sports drinks are very high in sugar and calories — it is important to know when to use [certain drinks], as well as which ones are beneficial to your performance" (Macey, n.d.).

Athletes can find sources of hydration in foods like the following healthy options:

- Oatmeal
- Fruits and vegetables
- Low-fat vanilla yogurt
- Low-fat milk

Fueling up Before Workouts

Athletes who skip meals can harm their bodies.

"If you begin skipping meals it sets your body back, and it will not be able to manage the workload and demands you place on it throughout the day," said Armstrong.

Regular meals and snacks are part of Armstrong's day. She eats snacks for both training and pleasure. She doesn't think denying temptation all the time is a good thing for athletes.

"On-the-bike snacking or fueling is also important. After 60 to 90 minutes of aerobic exercise your glycogen levels become depleted; it is important to refuel these energy stores if your training session is longer than this," Armstrong said.

She continued, "If I have a sweet tooth, my go-to is fruit; I make it the easy choice by stocking my refrigerator with a variety of choices. If I don't grab some fruit, some of my other favorites are yogurt, cheese, or a glass of chocolate milk."

Eat to Recover

Athletes looking to prepare their bodies from the inside out must plan for proper recovery.

Sleep and its importance for athletic recovery are covered in the previous chapter. However, decisions athletes make during the day about their diets can help the body recover more effectively at night.

Armstrong incorporates a focus on recovery into every workout.

She shared, "There is a 30-minute window post-training where I focus on my recovery. This is done through a protein drink or natural foods such as plain yogurt with honey or maple syrup. The larger meal can come within a few hours post workout."

POINTS TO REMEMBER

- An athlete's success requires proper nutrition for growth and continued development of muscles, mental function, and the immune system.
- The value of food for athletes should never be judged by how much attention it gets. Nutrition should be the logical application of what athletes know about themselves combined with the basic scientific benefits of food.

CHAPTER SIX

IMPROVE YOUR AWARENESS

JOURNALING

RICHARD KENT INSTRUCTS a group of high school students to create an entry in their journals. Some of them like it and furiously fill line after line. Some of them struggle, looking off into space lost in thought or boredom.

It might sound like an English class, but they sit on the soccer field after a big game.

Kent, a former English teacher, uses this opportunity to allow students to process and unpack the game that was just played. He guides them with a series of prompts to analyze the strengths and weaknesses, the team, and the opponent.

They are instructed to visualize adjustments that should be made for future games.

The players, even those who don't enjoy writing,

seem to take it seriously because they understand that journaling is real work that can make a difference in their game.

Kent uses journaling to organize his athletes' training goals and organize their reflections about their performance. His teams have even been known to write when journals are not available. One team used airsickness bags on a flight back from England.

Athletes in every sport and of every performance level can benefit from journaling to learn about themselves and their sport. Kent finds a correlation between each of the following activities and the benefits of writing about them:

- Watching and debriefing practice and game film
- Studying the team playbook
- Reading articles, blogs, websites, and books
- Making mistakes
- Listening to interviews with professional athletes
- Visualizing
- Competing
- Preparation, control, and routine
- Self-encouragement
- Balance and alignment
- Downtime and playfulness (Kent, 2014)

BENEFITS OF JOURNALING

Organization

Journals enable athletes to organize, plan, and reflect.

It's easy for an athlete to forget why exactly they are training. Journaling about goals and new strategies can help athletes organize their intentions to focus on the bigger picture.

Athletes can then use journals as evidence for further self-reflection. When an athlete records a daily workout and dietary intake for that day and then records a journal entry at the end of the day, the athlete can begin making connections between activity and outcome.

When journals are used as a tool of reference, athletes can begin to see their achievements and reflect upon how their hard work has paid dividends. They can also identify strategies that work during games or competition and those that did not.

Motivation

Journaling helps athletes learn about patterns of motivation, energy, and fatigue. They find out what they know and, more importantly, what they don't know.

Knowing that a journal entry will follow a workout or a game can help athletes stay the course and sustain motivation and commitment. The added accountability increases the likelihood that athletes will push themselves during training.

Journaling also increases the ability to self-regulate behavior to accomplish carefully planned goals. By putting off immediate gratification in favor of long-term accomplishments and benefits, athletes can see how this discipline pays off as time goes on.

Confidence

When it's time to compete, journals provide athletes the opportunity to reflect on how dedicated they were to their training commitments and have faith that they did everything to prepare themselves.

Positive thinking and confidence go hand in hand. Journals can be used to develop positive affirmations and develop strategies for deploying positive thinking.

Emotional balance

As athletes write, they connect further with their experiences and future experiences on the horizon. They are not only looking backward, but they are solving problems and learning about themselves. As athletes face negative emotions, they reduce anxiety and develop strategies to manage those emotions by increasing self-awareness. This naturally leads to development.

Journals lend perspective. Too often, athletes can obsess over a poor performance or training session. Journals help vent that frustration, put it behind them, and identify patterns before, during, and after a poor performance.

Venting frustration is an important element in maintaining emotional balance. Athletes might not want to share the challenges and even the achievements associated with their sport with family, friends, or even teammates. A journal can provide the perfect outlet for working through these emotions.

Physical balance

Journals can help athletes break through physical plateaus by evaluating performance and enhancing their future approach to achieve new levels of success.

Preventative and reflective efforts are also important in maintaining physical balance for athletes.

Journals can help prevent overtraining. When athletes become more aware of their physical state after a workout or competition through writing, they can recognize when it might be time to lighten up on training.

Journals can also provide insight into patterns that may have contributed to an injury.

DIFFERENT WAYS TO JOURNAL

There are many ways to journal. One size does not fit all. Athletes should feel free to use a variety of methods or stick with just one that works.

Simple bulleted lists. Include time and place of training and details like distance, reps, or sets. Rate your effort, energy levels, meals, sleep quality the night before, and motivation.

Preparation. Athletes can benefit from journals to prepare themselves for competition. Questions like the following can put you in the right frame of mind to achieve your personal best:

- What am I looking forward to?
- What am I grateful for?
- When something goes wrong, how am I going to react?
- How will I keep myself in the moment?
- What mantra or cue words am I going to call upon?

Reflection. Describe how the training felt. Include details about feelings afterward - both emotional and physical. Describe your thought process and recovery process, as well as any muscle soreness. Comment on the effects of nutritional variations on performance.

Prompts. A coach or trainer can provide prompts. Athletes can also find many prompts through a quick internet search, or they can develop their own.

- On days I'm not feeling my best, did I make a few bad eating decisions?
- Am I overestimating or underestimating my training?

- On days where I felt particularly focused and effective, what routine did I follow?
- How did my use of cue words work today? Where could I have used them but forgot?

Routine entries. Some athletes prefer a consistent approach that requires no creativity. They simply address the same items in each entry. For example, they might answer these three questions in each entry:

1. What worked well today?
2. What went wrong?
3. Anything else worth noting?

Free write. For some athletes, just writing in a stream-of-consciousness format is most effective. The entire entry does not have to be focused on the training or the competition. Elements from your personal life might very well be impacting your performance, so examining those issues and working through them can certainly be helpful.

Drawings or diagrams. Athletes who don't enjoy writing can supplement or replace words entirely with drawings or diagrams to reflect or prepare themselves for competition. This can be particularly effective for younger athletes.

PROFESSIONAL ATHLETES WHO JOURNAL

Curt Schilling. The Boston Red Sox pitcher has been known to record pitches to many batters and the effectiveness of those pitches in between innings. He includes details of the scenarios at work. Of course, he could reflect later by watching back the game, but recording his feelings at the moment likely provides additional insights that may have been lost if he had waited until after the game to reflect.

Serena Williams. During her victory at Wimbledon 2007, Williams shared a few pages of her journal. Some of the entries were as simple as only one sentence:

- "My good thoughts are powerful.
- My only negative thoughts are weak.
- Decide what you want to be, have, do and think thoughts of it.
- Hang on to the thought of what you want. Make it absolutely clear.
- You will look at balls.
- You will move up.
- You're #1.
- You are the best.
- You will add spin.
- Turn FAST.
- You will have long follow throughs.
- You will win Wimbledon" (Writing Athletes, n.d.).

LISTEN TO YOUR BODY

Receiving advice like "listen to your body" can feel nebulous. What does it mean?

It means having self-awareness, physically, mentally, and emotionally. Self-awareness means cultivating the ability to make yourself the subject of your awareness. Study after study over the past 50 years shows that attention can be focused outward on the environment or inward on yourself, but awareness cannot be focused on both at the same time.

To listen to your body, you need to develop the ability to become present and identify extremely subtle changes within yourself. This requires becoming aligned with yourself and attentive to your breathing, your heartbeat, your digestion, your mental state, and your physical state.

Successful athletes leave very little to chance for skill development, nutrition, or fitness, so why would you leave the more subtle aspects of the physical or mental game to chance? The more you know yourself, the more you can control yourself. The more variables you can control, the better control you're likely to have over your performance outcome.

It also means knowing your strengths and weaknesses inside and out and developing strategies that accentuate those strengths to compensate for those weaknesses. Tennis great Steffi Graf was doing this every time she ran around a backhand shot to maximize her forehand. You won't see Shaquille O'Neal going for many three-pointers instead of staying near the net to use his size and force to dunk on the opposition nearly every time.

When athletes learn how to do these things, they can learn what to expect before, during, and after training and competing. This can provide a sense of calm and control.

Make no mistake. This process is not a quick and easy one. Becoming introspective is difficult and takes time to master. When coaches ask questions like "What is holding you back?" many athletes have a hard time answering. Being honest about your weak spots is hard and requires real honesty and trust.

Listening to your body is particularly important when recovering from an injury. Too often, athletes want to speed up their recovery to avoid letting their teammates down. However, by going back to the game before the body is fully recovered, athletes can put themselves and their athletic careers at even higher risk. Listening to your body can help prevent this. Listen and trust what your body is telling you.

How Does It Work?

Identify your blind spots. Start by asking others - coaches, teammates, parents - for honest feedback. Ask them what you might be missing, both physically and mentally. Ask how you could be a better teammate. Ask what aspect of the game they think you can put more effort into. Watch videos and do some real self-assessment and reflection to understand their feedback.

Listen to your inner voice. We all run a script in our heads. What kind of self-talk do you hear? Is it positive and encouraging, or is it negative and chronically critical? When you learn something new or develop a new skill, what kind of script do you use to motivate yourself?

If you find that your inner voice is intensely negative, action needs to be taken to reframe that voice. First, you must identify when you tend to use negative self-talk. Is it under pressure? Is it after a mistake? Once you identify the patterns, replace negative self-talk with language that reflects a growth mindset. For example, instead of saying, "I suck at this," try tapping into a growth mindset that will sound more like "With practice and determination, I will improve." Try channeling the pressure that caused the negative self-talk in the first place into other pre-practice routines or other rituals.

Are you present? How effective are you at letting things go? When you make a mistake, are you holding on to it an hour later, or do you know how to let it go and stay present?

If you need work here, consider meditation. Focus is a mental muscle that requires practice and discipline just like any other muscle in the body. Find some quiet time and try just one minute of clearing your mind and breathing in and out. Try to think of nothing else except breathing in and out. When a random thought comes fluttering by - and it will - gently acknowledge it and guide your mind back to your breath. Eventually, with more practice, the amount of time between those fluttering thoughts will get longer and longer. As those periods extend, so will your ability to keep the mind in the present moment rather than focusing on a mistake you made in that last game.

Journals are a great tool to support this process.

AWARENESS

Many athletes expect the repetition of physical practice to develop the correct habits and ensure the right outcome.

If it were this easy, everyone would be a professional athlete.

The mind resists developing new habits. It doesn't like to do it. It often produces the wrong responses, and players who don't focus on awareness and training the mind will continue to miss the mark during competition and suffer by putting effort only towards physical practice.

For practice to be effective and result in improvement, athletes must focus on awareness. To become more aware, athletes need to identify their patterns of:

- Entertaining negative thoughts.
- Allowing the mind to be hijacked and controlled by the wrong emotions.
- Stifling the flow of positive energy or cutting

it off altogether by continuing without a
mental training strategy.

By operating using bad habits, athletes ingrain these habits into their physical performance and become their own worst enemies.

Have you ever had one of these negative thoughts:

- I can't beat this player, or we can't beat this team.
- We always lose when we play in this field.
- We always lose in overtime.
- When I fault on the first serve, I'm always less confident on the second one.
- I never have energy at evening practice.

Of course, you have had these thoughts. Every athlete has. Even though athletes might be ashamed to admit that these thoughts are ever entertained, it's human to have ideas like these and many others that enter your mind. We all know negative thinking can do irreparable damage to all of the time, energy, and effort put towards our athletic training. Athletes know negative thoughts can lead to negative performance. Unfortunately, negative thoughts are a part of life. It happens.

Here is the more important question: Are you aware of the thought when it occurs, how it persists, and how it impacts your attitude and performance?

Probably not so much.

When you become aware of these thoughts, you can

keep them at bay. What's more, you can cultivate habits that encourage positive thoughts to replace them. When athletes develop awareness around their thinking, they open up endless possibilities.

The journals that were discussed earlier are the perfect place to develop awareness.

Ask yourself at the beginning of each day, questions like:

- What challenges am I expecting today?
- How will I treat them when they present themselves?
- What positive attributes do I possess to solve problems that arise?
- In what other times in my life have I overcome obstacles?

Do it every day. Yes, every day. Even answering one of these questions will begin to develop the mental muscle for awareness. If you answer one question and only spend two minutes on it, your brain will begin to expect this kind of question at the beginning of the day. The more you make it routine, the more likely you will be to call upon these practical solutions when encountering negative thoughts.

When those negative thoughts enter your mind - and they will - be easy on yourself. Acknowledge the thought, congratulate yourself for recognizing it - even if it took an hour of letting it bounce around in your subconscious - and send it on its way.

Becoming aware of the negative thoughts is a huge first step to ridding yourself of their power over you as an athlete.

Once you can identify them, you can then begin replacing them with powerful positive thoughts like we discussed in Chapter 3.

Again, use that journal to prepare yourself with some positive thought replacements like:

- I need to think like a warrior to win.
- What positive things can I focus on right now?
- It's the better player who wins; it's the player who plays better.

That last thought leads to the next point about awareness.

Fixed Mindset vs. Growth Mindset

Becoming aware of how the brain operates and directing your thinking is another powerful strategy for athletes looking for more control over their performance.

Those with a growth mindset believe that ability can be developed. Athletes with a growth mindset understand that they can improve through hard work and create healthy habits and effective strategies.

Athletes with a fixed mindset believe that their athletic ability is a fixed trait that is mostly unchangeable.

An athlete's beliefs about their athletic ability have

significant consequences for how they experience training and competition, and how they respond to setbacks and adversity. Athletes with a fixed mindset can avoid challenges, give up more easily when faced with a struggle, and end their athletic careers because of false beliefs about their ability and potential.

Athletes with a growth mindset see challenges as opportunities to grow and are more likely to embrace those challenges to push themselves beyond current perceived limitations and thereby train harder and compete better.

Here are some examples.

Example 1

Put aside the fixed mindset, which says:

My teammates are using their time to get in extra weight lifting training, but I am too exhausted to do anything but go home and eat dinner.

Shift your focus to a growth mindset, and try:

It's okay that I'm not at that extra weight lifting session. What I need right now are food and rest. I'll get a good night's sleep, and I'll be able to join the extra session tomorrow.

Example 2

Instead of using the fixed mindset, which says:

I never make the starting lineup. My coach must think I'm just not good enough.

Shift your focus to a growth mindset, and try:

My coach just doesn't know what I'm capable of yet. I'm going to journal tonight and develop three new goals to achieve that will demonstrate my commitment to my coach and help him see me in a new light.

Example 3

Instead of using the fixed mindset, which says:

My batting average will never be as good as my teammate's batting average.

Shift your focus to a growth mindset, and try:

I can learn new strategies and new techniques to improve my batting average. I have made progress in being decisive and patient at the plate, and I can make the same progress with my swing. When I do make it on base, I add so much to the team as a base runner.

Being aware of these two mindsets will enable athletes to realize there is a choice. Becoming aware of choosing a growth mindset each day brings athletes closer to mastering control over more of their potential.

RESILIENCE

Awareness is particularly important when an athlete encounters a setback. Whether it is an injury, a goal left unachieved, or athletes must address a major loss, resilience, and the awareness of its importance.

Resilience isn't something we're born with. Some athletes were never taught about it, and even if they were, it isn't something that happens overnight. Resilience is a set of coping mechanisms that athletes develop over time. Performance is largely determined not by our circumstances or an athlete's genetic makeup but by an athlete's actions.

Some athletes just aren't aware of how much control they do have in how resilient they are or can be.

Again, resilience and awareness of it can be developed through journal writing. Writing about a setback, rather than just replaying it in your mind, can help make sense. By realizing that the setback hasn't caused the world to end and recognize your ability to maintain your daily routines, you develop your resilience.

Journaling about the path forward, the necessary steps to take, and where that path can lead is an integral part in the development of resilience. Journal entries don't need to be perfect. It's okay if you haven't figured out exactly what the next steps are. The important part is opening your mind to the possibilities instead of dwelling on the setback.

Sometimes the setback is so significant that progress may be difficult. Again, that's okay. Even if you do only one item each day to move forward, that is something. Being flexible is part of being resilient.

Gratitude also plays a part in resilience. Using your journal to list items for which you're grateful helps to play up those items and diminish the setback's effect by reducing feelings of hopelessness and powerlessness. Resilience is about maintaining hope and restoring power.

When working towards becoming more resilient in the face of a setback, don't be afraid to ask for help. Becoming a resilient athlete doesn't mean you have to handle everything alone. Talk to teammates or coaches to help reshape your perspective about the setback and the path forward.

THE IMPORTANCE OF BREATHING

Breathing. It's involuntary. It's something we do every day often without thinking. As a result, it often doesn't get the amount of attention it deserves when it comes to athletic performance. However, the benefits that proper breathing can provide are staggering and should not be overlooked.

When athletes concentrate on slower, more effective breathing on and off the field, they can experience tremendous results.

Reduced anxiety. The body is always striving to achieve homeostasis or equilibrium. Because athletic performance is continuously working against that equilibrium by pushing the body in and out of cardiorespiratory challenges, athletes can help achieve that equilibrium when at rest or off the field entirely through breathing. Athletes who practice meditation and deep breathing exercises can ward off anxiety, depression, insomnia, and digestive issues.

Improved focus. When breathing slows down intentionally, heart rhythms stabilize and allow the mind to focus. Consider pairing deep breathing exercises when practicing the visualization techniques previously discussed in the book.

Increased endurance. Athletes who practice breathing through a variety of very simple techniques will feel the difference at the end of the workout and in the last minutes of competition. Instead of losing steam and momentum, athletes will be able to push harder through the end.

Better blood flow. While stretching at the end of a workout, athletes who breathe properly increase the amount of blood pumped back into the heart. When this happens, the body experiences many benefits, including disposing of toxins and metabolic waste produced during the exertion of energy.

HOW CAN I DO IT?

There are several easy ways to incorporate proper breathing techniques into your training and competition playbook.

Six BPM. This is six breaths per minute. Pretty simple, right? This breathing rate promotes heart rate to increase inhalation and decrease respiration, resulting in a lower overall heart rate. The ultimate goal here is for athletes to be able to access this strategy during competition on demand. When they feel pressure, they simply pull up the go-to strategy to center their minds and move toward optimal performance.

Six BPM is the goal. Smaller steps will help athletes

get there. In all of the smaller steps breathing through the nose is the key to achieving the benefits of proper breathing.

Athletes who need a broken down strategy into smaller pieces can benefit from these simple exercises to build up to it over time.

Ten count. This simple technique helps beginners focus energy on their breath and get started with focusing on the practice of intentional breathing. Just like when you meditate, try to only focus on the breath.

Breathe in. Breathe out. One.

Breathe in. Breathe out. Two.

All the way to ten.

Try it.

If you got distracted, like many of us do at first, that's normal. Forgive yourself and try again.

Bend and breathe. Bend forward from your waist as far as you can in a comfortable way and place the palms of your hands on your lower back. As you inhale and exhale, see how many seconds you can count on each inhale and on each exhale.

Again, if you get distracted, just start over.

Head to toe. This is a breathing technique you can practice as you fall asleep. Lay on your back with your eyes closed. Slow your breathing. Focus your attention on your head. Dedicate one cycle of breath to focus on relaxing your forehead. Next, move to your eyes. Dedicate another cycle of breath here, noticing the tension in your eyes and intentionally let them relax. Continue this process with each cycle of breath. You might fall asleep, which is completely fine.

The ultimate goal here is to begin to train yourself to notice the breath and its power, so that come game time, you can call upon it to support you.

POINTS TO REMEMBER

- When athletes develop awareness around their thinking, they open up endless possibilities.
- When journals are used as a tool of reference, athletes can begin to see their achievements and reflect upon how their hard work has paid dividends.
- They can also identify strategies that work and those that do not.
- The more you know yourself, the more you can control yourself. The more variables you can control, the better control you're likely to have over your performance outcome.
- Athletes who become aware of negative thoughts can keep them at bay and cultivate positive thoughts to replace them.
- An athlete's beliefs about their athletic ability have significant consequences when it comes to how they experience training and competition and how they respond to setbacks and adversity.

CHAPTER SEVEN

BUILD YOUR NETWORK

ONCE THE LOS ANGELES LAKERS coach, Pat Riley, is infamous for conducting practice that is five times harder than the exertion during an actual game. Riley understood that games are won or lost in that last quarter, and the team with the endurance is likely to prevail.

In the old days, a coach could tell a team to run through a wall and do it. Today, athletes who are often treated like royalty need a different kind of motivation.

Even with the intense practice, Riley asked for 25% more from the players. The players pushed back, and Riley's team was about to go off the rails. Riley went to motivational coach Tony Robbins for help.

Robbins advised Riley to go back to the team and apologize. Gulp. Riley did not jump at this suggestion at first. He did not like the idea, but he followed the advice of Robbins.

Riley apologized and told the team that they really couldn't get much better. Following Robbins' advice, he asked for just 1% more. The players looked at each other and scoffed at the 1%, knowing they were capable of much more, as if to say *we can do way better than that, watch us*.

Having a coach or a trainer who is willing to seek advice from others, swallow their pride, apologize, and try new strategies is essential. Building a network of people on whom you can rely can be the difference between a career that thrives and fizzles.

SURROUND YOURSELF WITH THE RIGHT TRAINING PARTNERS

In the past few decades, group training has become an international trend as spin cycling, aerobic, and dance-based exercise classes have all become wildly popular. The emergence and rapid success of concepts like CrossFit indicate how effective exercising with a pack mentality can enhance athletic performance.

Research shows that healthy exercise habits, decisions, and actions of others can be a very good influence. Athletes gravitate towards the exercise behaviors of those around them. Surrounding yourself with those who make good decisions and those who are a few steps ahead of you is a good idea.

Surrounding yourself with the right people is important in all walks of life, especially in your athletic development. Exercising with someone else is good.

Exercising with someone more advanced than you is even better.

Here are five questions to ask yourself when considering who is the best training partner for you.

1. Is this person's ability level similar to mine?
2. Can I learn from this person's strengths?
3. Do this person and I have similar goals?
4. Does this person have the right attitude?
5. Does this person train the way I want to train (this question is not about whether the person trains the way I train now, but how I want to train in my ideal world)?

The Benefits

Drive commitment. Of course, you will look for training partners that give as much as you do, and maybe even more. You'll have more energy to face athletic challenges when support goes both ways.

When you work out with the right people, you will experience benefits that drive motivation, consistency, and duration. When you work out with others, it's likely part of an implied contract. You have committed to showing up with your best effort for one another. Positive peer pressure from others will increase your commitment to training.

Athletes are typically committed to their development, but sometimes it can be not easy to achieve consistency and maximize commitment to training schedules and routines. When athletes have training partners depending on them, accountability kicks in, and commitment levels rise.

Intensify effort. You would likely agree that nobody wants to be the weakest link in a group setting. This idea has a name. It is called the Kohler effect. For athletes and those exploring fitness, the Kohler effect means you are more likely to push yourself harder when working out with people who are more advanced or fit.

A study proved that those who worked out with a more capable partner improved their best plank time by 24%. The motivational gain of the more competent partner pushed the participants in the study beyond limits that otherwise would have held them back.

In every group, there is always that person who becomes the 'reach' or the 'goal' for the group.

You are likely to work out longer and harder if you are working out with the right people. Studies by the Society of Behavioral Medicine confirm that working out with a partner improved performance and time spent exercising. Results were even better for those who worked out with a group in a team format. Some doubled their workout time compared to those who exercised alone.

Highly effective athletes opt for group workouts a few times per week to push themselves toward their personal best efforts and outcomes.

Grab that competitive edge. Let's be honest. When your teammate, friend, or even a stranger is running beside you, the inherently competitive nature inside every athlete causes you to push yourself harder. This kind of competitiveness is positive.

You can become inspired to work harder, do more, and even find new ways to exercise. You might also learn something about yourself that you hadn't previously realized. You may have avoided trying a new routine or strategy, but working out with others helps you learn to be more flexible and willing to pivot. This can open the door for substantial growth opportunities.

Exponentially boost endorphins. Workouts with others are more fun. Someone is likely to yell some encouraging words. A little encouragement goes a long way during a workout. A few shouts from partners to do one more rep or one more quarter mile can be just what you need. When one of the weaker group members is having an especially good day, the positive vibes begin flowing and become infectious. The mental advantages of a group workout are great for morale. You've heard of the runner's high and already know that working out, even when alone, boosts endorphins. When you add the social element of a group workout, now you are releasing endorphins in different ways.

You are more likely to smile around others, and that boosts endorphins.

Someone tells a joke during a workout, and that boosts endorphins.

The above mentioned additional commitment and intensified effort that results from working out with others make you feel better and more accomplished. That also boosts endorphins.

Provide new perspectives. Seeing training, progress, and competition from different points of view can support resilience and awareness. Surrounding yourself with partners and teammates with a positive attitude helps you focus on the possibility of growth. Partners also see you differently than you see yourself and can help you gain the confidence to break outdated or unwanted habits and patterns. They can also help you visualize possibilities.

Relieve stress. Social support has been studied and proven to be a powerful predictor of happiness, health, longevity, success, and resilience. Surrounding yourself with the right people as you train and compete can act as a buffer to reduce stress and promote your ability to cope with challenges.

The personal connections we make with others are suitable for the soul. When athletes train with teammates or workout partners, they report feeling calmer and enjoying the workout more than when training alone. Time flies when you are having fun, so the group workout is likely to last longer and provide you with added stress relief and endurance.

Diversify your routine. Variety is said to be the spice of life. The same holds for athletic training. Training partners bring fresh new ideas to a workout, but working out in pairs or groups extends the spectrum of exercises possible. You can now make more moves like medicine ball toss sit-ups and relay cardio routines.

You now have someone to heighten the safety of your

workout by spotting you. Still, you can lift a heavier load, and you also have someone to troubleshoot your form and help you realign to achieve your best results.

Avoid training partners that are reluctant to expand their horizons. You need partners who will help you look for new ways to develop as an athlete. Since it's exactly those new strategies, exercises, and approaches that forge new brain connections that enable you to push through plateaus and adapt when faced with a setback, these are the types of partners you are seeking.

Add accountability. Athletes who train with others often report being able to accomplish things they never thought were possible until a training partner or teammate pushed them through a physical or emotional plateau. Athletes create a bond with one another because pushing yourself involves a certain degree of vulnerability. Exposing this part of oneself develops camaraderie that leads to accountability that is always good for overall athletic achievement.

FAMILY AND FRIENDS

One of the most famous athletes of all time, Tiger Woods, was trained from a young age by his father. Earl Woods used many different strategies with Tiger, one of which was cursing quite explicitly during Tiger's backswing. It might be an unorthodox approach, but Tiger swears it helped him enormously throughout his golf career and even through personal trials and tribulations. Earl Woods knew Tiger would have to maintain an unparalleled focus to become competitive and successful. Tiger often claims to see but not see and to hear but not hear because of those exercises.

Michael Jordan's family also had a significant impact on his work ethic and his athletic perseverance. His father, a maintenance worker, built Jordan a basketball court in the backyard of their home. His mother, a bank teller, was the rule enforcer and instilled the drive to succeed in her son. Larry Jordan, Michael's older brother, gets credit for the all-star's competitive side. The two played out back on that court until bedtime every day.

Jordan Spieth finds support from his family in a different way. He can appreciate the game no matter how he plays. Spieth attributes this attitude of gratitude, which helps take the pressure off, to having a sister with special needs. Her ability to be happy despite the struggles she faces helps him maintain perspective and realize how lucky he is to tee it up for a living.

These are the success stories.

We know that not every player will be the next Tiger Woods, Michael Jordan, or Jordan Spieth. Unfortunately, many parents have yet to realize this fact.

Parent Involvement in Youth Sports

It is all too often that signs at youth athletic fields have to remind parents of the proper ways to behave at their children's sporting events. Signs display instructions like:

1. These are kids.
2. This is a game.
3. The coaches are volunteers.
4. The umpire is human.
5. Your kid does not play for the Yankees.

In the past few decades, sports have become an opportunity for parents to live vicariously through their children. Sports are also seen as an investment to many parents, many of whom believe this investment may lead to a college scholarship. Parents start their kids in sports earlier and earlier. Some even begin as toddlers, next playing on expensive travel teams, and spending a large portion of childhood traveling to and from private coaching, practice, and competitive tournaments.

Life in many aspects is all about keeping up with the Joneses, and youth sports are no different for many parents.

There are many different arguments for and against this new approach to youth sports. The most significant question parents should ask is: What does my child want?

A recent study at George Washington University surveyed nearly 150 children about what they found fun about sports and why so many are quitting. Kids identified 81 factors contributing to their happiness. You can probably guess that tournament play and expensive equipment was low on the list. Positive team dynamics, learning, and positive coaching topped the list.

Parents and coaches often don't want to hear about these types of findings.

Parent Involvement in Olympic Sports

Olympic athletes can turn to people outside of their team and training circle for support. Friends and family members can provide emotional and mental backup, but they can also cause emotional and mental strain.

The 2008 U.S. Olympic diving team knows this first hand. One of the coaches, Chris Carr, is now a sports and performance psychologist. Carr and his colleagues held workshops for divers' family and friends before the Olympics to teach them how to optimize support and minimize distraction.

As elite athletes train to become Olympians, their parents often require just as much training to transform themselves into Olympians' parents. Sports psychologists don't only support the athletes anymore. Sports psychologists also counsel the athletes' families to develop a family dynamic that nurtures the athlete's performance and achievement and maintains their emotional balance.

Parents can struggle to figure out what the best type and amount of involvement looks like. Parents know how to provide financial support and logistical support for their athletes, but the emotional support piece is the tricky. Parents often fall into one of two situations:

- When athletes struggle with physically, psychologically, and emotionally demanding

schedules, pressure, and responsibilities, parents can find themselves unequipped or unprepared to help.
- Other parents might over provide, and their support might extend to an unhealthy approach or amount that piles on top of the stress the athlete is already under. Parents who blur the line between where they end and where the athlete's life begins can become a distraction for their children.

Sports psychologists can help parents maintain their composure and provide athletes with tools to help parents if that is the most effective. Parents should be optimistic and supportive of their children. Leave the performance, the score, and the standings to the coach.

SEEK PROFESSIONAL HELP

Sports Psychologists

Athletes have a different mindset than they once did.

Have you ever seen a character in an action film who gets an electrical shock and is blasted across the room?

It's easy to think that the shock is what propelled that person across the room. In reality, the electrical impulse causes all the fibers in the body's muscles to twitch at once. The body throws itself across the room.

That tells you something about the amount of power contained in the human body.

How does this relate to sports psychologists?

The brain acts as a limiter to that power and essentially prevents us from accessing all of that power. It might be a natural protectant, so we don't hurt ourselves by tearing muscles and ligaments.

The more we learn about the brain and how it limits the human body, the more we become able to peel back those limits.

Sports psychologists help athletes to convince the brain to peel back its limits.

Endurance activity was once thought to be harmful to the body. Still, now we know that the body is designed for endurance. This knowledge inspires athletes toward bigger and more challenging feats.

Sports psychologists change the mindset of athletes and open the door for athletes to understand what they are truly capable of.

Sports Physiologists

Sports physiologists study how physical activity affects the body. Coaches and trainers are sometimes physiologists, but some athletes work with physiology specialists. These professionals can help athletes optimize performance, recover from injury, prevent injury, and learn proper technique.

The role of physiology can contribute to the optimal preparation for athletes. Athletes undergo a series of tests in a climate-controlled environment chamber. The physiologists can adjust the climate to reflect what the athlete is likely to encounter during competition. For example, athletes competing in the Summer Olympics in the southern hemisphere will test in temperatures within the range for the predicted time of year.

Based on test results, physiologists can advise athletes how to train optimally and advise coaches to adjust training schedules accordingly. Physiologists will collate specific test results for each athlete that ultimately contribute to the design of optimal workouts for that particular athlete.

For example, the tests might include:

- Checking how much sweat is lost in certain climate conditions.
- Attaching sweat patches to see which chemicals in which amounts are present in the sweat to adjust hydration strategies to maintain fluid balance and electrolyte levels.
- Assessing which energy sources are utilized during exercise.
- Testing gas exchange to measure thresholds for physical preparedness and peak performance.
- Analyzing pulmonary oxygen uptake to determine how much oxygen is being used and how much carbon dioxide is being produced in various scenarios to understand the burn ratio of carbohydrates to fat.

- Employing near-infrared devices that analyze how proteins deliver oxygen to the body to identify what exercise intensity does to various muscle groups.

All of this data is then used to prescribe the most effective training routine.

POINTS TO REMEMBER

- Surrounding yourself with the right people is important in all walks of life, but especially so in your athletic development.
- Having a coach, trainer, or training partner who is willing to seek advice from others, swallow their pride, apologize, and try new strategies is essential.
- Parents know how to provide financial support and logistical support for their athletes—take care with emotional support.
- Sports psychologists can help parents maintain their composure and can also provide athletes with tools to help their parents if required.
- The more we learn about the brain and how it powers and limits the human body, the more we can fuel that power and peel back those limits.

CHAPTER EIGHT

BELIEVE IN YOURSELF

ANDRE AGASSI WAS one of the first athletes that worked with Tony Robbins. He had been number one in the world and won Wimbledon. He then experienced a fall from grace when he injured his wrist and then encountered a series of losses. He was considering quitting the sport.

Tony Robbins worked with Agassi. Agassi was skeptical. Robbins asked if Agassi had ever hit a tennis ball perfectly. He asked him to visualize himself, hitting the ball perfectly ten times. Robbins watched as Agassi, with eyes closed, began to smile as he envisioned this. Agassi said he was not thinking about his wrist at all as he visualized.

They both watched a video of Agassi winning at Wimbledon. They watched Agassi walk onto the court with complete confidence. Robbins called his body language prowling. Agassi admitted that he was thinking to himself about his opponent, "Why did you even show up?"

Robbins and Agassi then watched a video of Agassi after a series of losses. The body language had changed. Robbins pointed out that Agassi was not the same man.

Robbins was trying to prove that the athlete with greater certainty and confidence will always achieve greater success.

HOW DO YOU ACHIEVE CERTAINTY?

Physiology and focus play a role that is greater than most people realize.

Energy makes that difference. To shift energy, athletes must create momentum. Once you create or change momentum, your game will change.

You take action, and you believe it will happen. Close the gap between potential and results by understanding that certainty is everything.

Too often, you can see an athlete walk out onto the field and know whether they have certainty or don't.

Consider this example. A kicker walks out onto the field to kick a field goal. He has little certainty. The body language reflects it. The ability to execute is deflated.

This chapter will examine how that kicker can change the results in advance by using his mind to change his state.

WHAT IS SELF-CONFIDENCE?

If you sometimes feel that everyone but you is sure of themselves and confident, you are not alone. It's very likely that these people doubt themselves and have insecurities.

So why do they seem so confident?

The answer is likely straightforward. They realize that confidence is not about knowing it all or a trait that you have, but it is something that you work hard to create. Being confident is the certainty that you can accomplish anything you set your mind and energy to.

There is a certain level of trust you must have in yourself to believe - believe - that you can navigate your way to a successful outcome regardless of the situation.

WHAT ARE THE BENEFITS OF BEING SELF-CONFIDENT?

Perseverance. During those times, when athletes feel like giving up, confidence can be the lifeline that pulls them through. Confidence gets you through the toughest training, the games where your team is trailing, the times where you are simply outmatched by an opponent, or when a teammate takes your spot on the roster.

Perception. Coaches and teammates don't look to athletes who are consistently unsure of themselves. To be a productive part of any team, you need to present confidence during even the most difficult of situations.

Relationship building. By fostering maturity and overcoming insecurity, confidence will help athletes handle relationship conflicts with teammates, trainers, and coaches, and solve problems that arise.

HOW TO IMPROVE SELF-CONFIDENCE

To become more confident, you must change your state.

Athletes, like all other human beings, have emotional patterns. Your state is your mental or emotional pattern at any given point in time. These mental or emotional conditions tend to influence the way we see life.

The great news is that you can change your state anytime, anywhere, no matter what.

Learning to change your state is one of the greatest - and simplest - gifts an athlete can give themselves.

You need to know how to do it.

THE STORY

The first step is the story we all tell ourselves. We all have that story. We tell ourselves what we are really like, what we are capable of, and where our limits begin. We tell ourselves we can do these things, but not those. The dangerous or powerful part about this is that we are usually right. It all comes down to the story that we tell ourselves. The great news is that you are in charge of that story.

Tell yourself a story where the things you hope for

and dream about are possible, and you're usually going to be right.

Tell yourself a story where those things are out of your reach, or you don't deserve them, and guess what? You're usually going to be right.

You know those people who say, "I'm just not a runner." They never became runners, did they?

Don't let your story limit you. Let your story lift your state and your certainty about what you can achieve.

Here is the question: If you have the freedom to write your own story, what will you write?

The Strategies

Body language. Think of someone you consider to be unwaveringly confident. How would you describe them? When they enter a room, how do they behave? How do they carry themselves? How do they walk? What kind of eye contact do they make? What type of posture do they have?

For those seeking confidence, the phrase "fake it until you make it" can get the ball rolling. In other words, act like you're confident. Right now, try it. Stand up straighter, pull your shoulders back, and control your breathing. Mastering your body language is critical to becoming more confident.

Your physiology can radically change your mood, your state, and your confidence.

Positive thinking. Where your focus goes, your

energy tends to follow. What you focus on becomes bigger. These are all sayings that you have probably heard before. Do you know why you've heard them? You've heard them because they are true.

The mind can only focus on a small piece of experience. The good news is that you can condition your brain to seek the positive pieces of your experience.

Consider when you buy a new pair of running sneakers, and all of a sudden, you begin to notice those sneakers everywhere. Did everyone buy them when you did? Of course not. Your brain has been conditioned to look for them by spending a small amount of time concentrating on them during purchase.

The mind's reticular activating system (RAS) programs your brain to pay attention to certain things. Mental conditioning helps lead the RAS in paying attention to the positive visualization elements you are seeking. The RAS acts as a customs checkpoint and determines what is going to get through to your mind and what is going to be turned away.

Try it. Think about an upcoming practice. Let's say you had your best sprint time ever, but also had a problem with a coach at the last practice. The piece of that memory on which you choose to focus will become bigger in your mind. Give it a try.

Focus on the sprint time. You see yourself running. You feel your blood pumping, hear your heart beating, feel the wind on your face, and the exhilaration of beating your personal best time. You're probably feeling pretty good right about now.

Now focus on the problem with your coach. Relive the argument, your side of the story, and how you may have been understood. Feeling some anxiety building up? You're probably not feeling so great.

When you practice daily conditioning to decide what you want, you can begin to use your mind and positive thinking as a conditioning tool, just like you would a muscle-building supplement.

How can you do this?

Use affirmations paired with physical movement and feeling to create a level of certainty in your entire body. Decide what you want and condition yourself daily. Find role models. Write down the specific skills that you are seeking to develop or improve. Then seek out role models - either those you know or professional athletes that you can read about - and do what they do. Decide to commit on a large scale and in an intelligent way.

What you focus on becomes bigger. Again, the great news is that you are in control of that choice.

Positive thinking can manifest itself in different ways. Instead of obsessing about how things might go wrong, focus your attention and visual imagery on all the good things.

Replace negative images, predictions, and self-talk with more positive thoughts and seek out the best possibilities when your mind begins working.

When you change your focus, you are changing the future by changing your state.

Growth mindset. A fixed mindset thinks that your skillset is, as the name indicates, fixed, and nothing can be done to change it. A growth mindset thinks that your skillset is dynamic and can be changed over time.

The fixed mindset thinks, "I suck at this." The growth mindset thinks, "With practice, I can improve and do better in the future."

Many people think that confidence develops from prior experiences - prior success in particular. The misconception that you can only be confident after you've achieved success is incorrect and severely limiting. Sure, confidence can be strengthened through success, but it initially comes from within.

Operating with a growth mindset means knowing that when you fail, you can and will brush yourself off and try again as many times as it takes.

Gratitude. When was the last time you stopped to be thankful for your body and your health that make it possible to be an athlete? How about being thankful that you live in a place in the world where it is safe enough to participate in recreational activities like athletics?

Practicing gratitude can help develop confidence in several ways.

First, how you feel about yourself affects the way you behave. When you appreciate all that is positive about yourself, you naturally build healthy self-esteem and confidence.

Second, gratitude boosts confidence by decreasing the potential for envious feelings or jealousy. Instead of wanting the winning record of a rival team or the starting spot on your team, you focus more on yourself and what is within your control and begin to recognize and focus on the progress only you can influence.

This is a perfect opportunity to use your journal. A gratitude journal is an ideal place to record three items each day for which you are grateful. For example:

1. A coach that goes out of her way to play motivational music for us.
2. The smell of the freshly cut grass at practice today.
3. Feeling my muscles relax as we stretched after practice and being grateful I have no injuries or pain.

Visualize success. Even the most seemingly confident people experience times of insecurity and doubt. When you notice these feelings begin to creep in, visualize a recent accomplishment or a future event having a wildly successful outcome. See yourself being as confident as possible and know that executing in that manner is well within your reach.

Power pose. We all have inner power. Athletes can increase confidence by tapping into that inner power. During times of uncertainty, remind yourself of this power by having a power pose at the ready.

Develop the pose that helps you reconnect with your inner power. Yoga poses like Warrior One or Warrior Two are especially effective. If you're not a yogi, try either of these easy poses:

- Standing with your hands on your hips and your feet shoulder-width apart.
- Standing with your head held high, your back straight, and your arms stretch high overhead.

The pose itself is not as important as the deep breaths you take and the positive images you visualize as you strike the pose to connect with your inner strength.

Breathing. Stress is a drain on an athlete's confidence. Stress and toxins can be alleviated by taking a full deep breath. Take an intentional deep breath that fills your lungs and slowly release the breath. By doing this simple act, athletes can radically decrease the stress and anxiety that can be draining on energy and confidence.

EXERCISES TO INCREASE CONFIDENCE

Exercise 1: High-Low Table

Understanding what causes your confidence to fluctuate is important in achieving greater confidence stability.

- Divide a piece of paper into two columns, labeling the first column, "high-confidence situations," and the second "low-confidence situations."

- In the first column, list situations in your sport where you feel entirely confident.
- In the second column, list the situations in which you lack confidence.

Exercise 2: The Spotlight

Visualizing your state during successful experiences in which you have felt high degrees of confidence can help maintain those feelings and help you tap into them during times of insecurity.

- Imagine a spotlight shining down a few feet in front of you.
- See yourself in the spotlight performing in one of the situations from the first column in the previous exercise.
- Visualize yourself performing at your peak level of athletic performance. As we discussed earlier, explore each of your senses.

Exercise 3: Positive Affirmations

Positive affirmations, or self-talk, will deepen your confidence. Knowing that you believe in yourself and your skills and abilities is a simple step that many athletes overlook.

- Develop statements that you truly believe about yourself. Examples include:

"Nobody's getting by me" (defensive linesman); "Just me and the catcher's mitt" (baseball pitcher); "Be aggressive" (baserunner)
- Practice whichever affirmations you choose before bed and when you wake in the morning. Repeat them as you train and in the shower. Use them as a distraction from negative thoughts or in times of anxious feelings.
- Most importantly, use them during games or competitions.

Exercise 4: Spin the Mix

Music can calm the savage beast. It can also inspire, motivate, and boost confidence. Athletes from all sports utilize music to help improve their confidence and performance.

Whether you are motivated by the lyrics, the beat, or other associations, music is a healthy athletic tool.

Athletes choose music to instill confidence in different ways. Consider variables like:

- Is there music that reminds you of an optimal past result?
- What is speaking to you at this particular moment?
- Which songs pump you up? Which songs calm you down?

- What works for teammates? What works for top athletes?

The key to choosing the right music for you is understanding how you need the music to motivate you. Then test your choices while warming up or during practice. See what makes you feel confident and ready to tackle whatever comes your way.

ANCHORING

You have likely heard about Pavlov and his dog. Pavlov conditioned dogs to drool whenever he would ring a bell. This was possible because the dogs became conditioned to associate the bell with food.

Pavlov was using a technique of Neuro-Linguistic Programming, or NLP. NLP is learning to speak the language that appeals to your particular mind. In essence, Pavlov was speaking the dog's language and creating deep associations between cause and effect.

NLP considers the conscious mind to be responsible for goal setting and the subconscious mind responsible for goal getting.

Within NLP is a strategy called anchoring, which enables you to create associations that have a motivational effect on your mind.

You probably have a song that makes you feel psyched and motivated to practice. That song is the anchor to accessing that motivation in your mind. Anchoring provides you with the chance to place an emotional order, just like at a restaurant. You want something, you order it, and it comes. By creating your anchors, you can create desired emotional outcomes.

Imagine being able to create a feeling of total calm and a feeling of centeredness by merely pushing your thumb and pointer finger together. Replace calm with whatever emotion you'd like and replace the physical stimulus of pushing fingers together with any other stimulus you'd love.

That is anchoring.

When athletes have an intense emotional experience and can identify and associate a specific stimulus with that experience, they can fire connections between those two things. The stimulus must be repeatedly used to create a strong connection between the feeling and the stimulus.

Here are a few examples.

Motivation for Amateur Runners

Imagine someone trying to get themselves in shape. Despite knowing that running is an effective solution for weight loss, this person has always perceived running as an oppressive workout and has found it difficult to begin a running routine.

This person sees two sets of grandparents with their grandkids. One set of grandparents has a hard time physically getting around. The other set of grandparents has always been physically fit. Seeing the physically fit grandparents changes the way the new runner sees fitness.

She creates the following mantra: *I'm creating a physically fit future for my kids, my grandkids, and myself.*

Every time she wakes up early to put on her running clothes, she says:

I'm creating a physically fit future for my kids, my grandkids, and myself.

Every time she opens the door to step outside - whether it's raining, freezing, or a beautiful day, she says:

I'm creating a physically fit future for my kids, my grandkids, and myself.

When she comes to the one-mile point, where she typically stops running and begins walking, she says:

I'm creating a physically fit future for my kids, my grandkids, and myself.

When the sweat is pouring down, and she wants to quit, she says:

I'm creating a physically fit future for my kids, my grandkids, and myself.

Her anchor, this mantra, becomes associated with powering through a run. Soon, all she has to do is silently repeat these words to herself. She can trigger the emotional reaction that motivates her into action.

Confidence for Competition

Think of a time during competition when you were confident. A time when you felt powerful. A time when you had not one doubt in your mind. Use your visualization skills to bring every feeling back. Make a fist. Think more about the confident experience. Make a fist. Repeat again and again.

Give yourself some space - maybe an hour. Test yourself by clenching your fist. If you've anchored effectively, you should feel those same confident emotions coming back.

If you're not there yet, be patient. Continue the anchoring process by visualizing and clenching your fist over and over until the test is successful.

That is how simple anchoring is.

Imagine walking up to the batter's box or the free-throw line and simply clenching your fist to fill yourself with confidence whenever you need it. It can be the difference between winning and losing, and more importantly, between success and failure.

How effective the anchor depends on the intensity of the experience you choose to focus on and the consistency at which it's called upon.

Imagine if you could call up states of motivation and confidence just like that. Consider the possibilities.

What difference could anchoring make in your athletic career? What about in your personal life?

RESOURCEFUL STATE

Many athletes unknowingly walk around with equipment that they have never tapped into. Human beings have natural capacities that can enable them to function at optimal levels and maximize their potential.

The bad news is that most human beings spend too much time operating in a non-resourceful state and end up blocking all of that potential. This non-resourceful state puts us in a rut where we feel like life is a constant struggle, and we might never get to the life we want to have. We work so hard to get to the destination that we don't know how to enjoy the journey.

However, there is good news. The good news is that we can put ourselves into what experts call a resourceful state essentially any time we want. It's like having the ability to flip a switch and transport ourselves to a place where we think more clearly, make better decisions, and live a life that leaves us feeling proud and energetic.

There's even more good news. Getting yourself in a resourceful state is not dependent on circumstances or recent events. You don't have to be performing at your best, winning, or super confident. You don't even have to be on the right track. When it comes to creating a state, you are entirely in control of generating this power. You bring magic to the situation.

Let's clarify. Being in a resourceful state is different from using positive thinking. Being in a resourceful state means changing your mindset so you don't have to convince yourself. You change the way you think so that you know that you can achieve anything, and you feel it throughout your body, heart, and mind. You feel it within every area of your life - your physical life, your emotional life, and your mental life.

You might be thinking that this sounds too good to be

true. If it's available and possible, why isn't everyone doing it?

Sadly, the answer is because the old fashioned way of thinking still dominates athletics. Hard work, putting your nose to the grindstone, and slugging through the challenges with nothing more than willpower and stamina are the answers.

Those things are all very worthwhile. But, there is another strategy that will make all of those things so much easier to achieve.

How To Get There

If you're in a bored state, you're going to feel bored.

If you're in a fearful state, you're going to feel afraid.

If you're in a confident state, you're going to feel confident.

Tony Robbins tells the story that when he was 17-years-old, he was living in his car, wondering what the next day would bring. Rather than letting himself remain in a fearful or insecure state, he made radical changes in his physiology and his mental inputs to change his state. He began reading autobiographies about wildly successful people who had overcome similar obstacles. He began training his body because he had learned that fear is physical. Going for a run or lifting weights would automatically diminish fear.

Step 1: **Change Your Physiology**

There is an acronym ACE, which is helpful to understand.

Action Changes Emotions.

Emotions are difficult to change, or so many think.

Actions are quite a bit easier to control.

Make a radical change in your body, and you make a drastic change in your state.

If you change your state, you change your life.

Try it right now. It's impossible to feel depressed if your body is behaving like it's happy. Go ahead. Try it. Put a smile on your face. Pull your shoulders back. Get up and do ten meaningful jumping jacks. While this is all happening, try to feel depressed. You can't do it.

This is the secret to changing your state.

Let's say it again: Change your state, change your life.

Step 2: Change Your Focus

Give yourself a few minutes at the start of every day to deliberately decide what you will focus on. When you focus and guide your mind, you make it more difficult for the mind to autopilot over to the land of worry and fear.

Need some ideas?

- **Gratitude.** Let's go back to the idea of gratitude again. Focus on finding three specific and unique things about the day for which you are truly grateful. When you focus on gratitude, it's very difficult to experience

fear. When you focus on gratitude, it's very difficult to experience jealousy.
- **Intention.** Call upon those new visualization skills. See yourself accomplishing what you are setting out to accomplish for the day.

Post reminders in your car if you need to. Post reminders in your kitchen, your office, whatever it takes to maintain that focus.

By doing this, you will rewire your habits.

Most people want to be happy, but their habits are wired to lead them into feelings of worry, stress, anger, etc. It's like designing a high-speed train to the land of stress and then using a horse-drawn carriage with a broken wheel on a dirt road to get to the land of happiness.

Step 3: Ask Yourself Habitual Questions

On that highway to stress are road signs with questions like:

Why do bad things always happen to me?

What does he have that I don't?

Why is she able to perform so much more consistently than I can?

To change your state, we need to reprogram the inner voice that we all use. One way to do that is by designing and making a habit of asking and answering productive and resourceful-state-centered questions like:

What am I grateful for today?
How many amazing physical gifts have I been given?
What can I do to improve my situation?
How can I take advantage of all the opportunities in front of me?

By asking ourselves questions that set us up for success, we train our minds to work for us rather than against us. We begin dismantling that highway to stress and start paving the road to peace and happiness.

POINTS TO REMEMBER

- Confidence is not about knowing it all or a trait that you have, but something that you work hard to create. Being confident is the certainty that you can accomplish anything you set your mind and energy to.
- By fostering maturity and overcoming insecurity, confidence helps athletes handle relationship conflicts with teammates, trainers, and coaches, and solve problems that arise.
- To become more confident, athletes must change their state.
- Athletes who practice daily conditioning can begin to use positive thinking as a conditioning tool, just like they would a muscle-building supplement.

CONCLUSION

Too many athletes at one point or another in their athletic careers find themselves stuck. They hit a physical plateau in their training, and they can't seem to find a way to improve, or they hit a mental plateau and begin to lose motivation.

When athletes find themselves stuck in this way, they start searching for answers. The critical element in that search is the source.

The internet contains massive amounts of information, but it has become increasingly clear that much of it is worthless because it lacks scientific backing and vetting. It could be a very legitimate program, but it's not right for your particular mental, emotional, or physical makeup. It might not address the underlying issue that is holding you back from pushing through and achieving success.

Some athletes turn to what is commonly being

referred to as bro-science. These are techniques or trends that might make an athlete get stronger and look better. Still, upon taking the field to train, practice, or compete, the athlete quickly realizes the effort did nothing for performance. Maybe the extra muscle even makes the athlete feel sluggish and harms performance.

Constructing a plan that will provide real momentum in your athletic career requires you to develop long term strategies that are custom made for you and the particular challenges you face every day in your training and competition.

It can be difficult for athletes to dig deep into the challenges at hand to discover what is getting in the way. Take a step away from all of the big exciting moments in sports - the moments of exhilaration, speed, and accomplishments - to examine yourself as an athlete. Why you do what you do, where you are right now, where you want to go, and how to get there are serious questions. By developing new habits, athletes will uncover these answers and draw insights to unleash potential that they never knew.

RECAP

Throughout this book, you have read about the eight habits adopted by numerous professional athletes. Let's quickly recap each of them.

Set Goals and Develop a Plan. Developing a plan helps athletes to build the capacity to focus their energies. By taking the extra few minutes to write down goals, athletes can increase their chances of achieving success.

Stay Consistent and Focused. Being able to focus is one thing. Focusing in the right way and on the right things is another. Successful athletes have realized that consistently engaging in preparatory rituals promote excellent performance. This is critical as athletes need to be able to trust practice and training to take over during competition. When a mistake is made in competition, it is critically important to let it go immediately.

Visualization and Mental Training. What sets apart the athletes who will find real success is mental toughness. When athletes visualize, they purposefully and intentionally rehearse a skill, a routine, or a play in their mind's eye in order and feel the process of creating a successful outcome. They tap into the part of the brain that is later going to perform the actual physical activity. Research proves that the mental activities athletes use to prepare themselves are just as important as the physical elements. When athletes see themselves becoming stronger, faster, and more skilled, the mind helps the body make it happen.

Sleep, Rest, and Recovery. Athletes know that what can be measured can be managed. Coaches must understand the physical and psychological benefits that rest and recovery after training and competition provide. With an increased focus on and an understanding of incorrect perceptions surrounding recovery, athletes can adjust habits and improve performance and overall well-being.

Healthy Eating and Fueling the Body. Athletes often lack specific nutritional knowledge, making it difficult to separate valid information from incorrect information. An athlete's success requires proper nutrition for growth and continued development of muscles, mental function, and the immune system. Nutrition should be the logical application of what athletes know about themselves combined with the basic scientific benefits of food.

Improving Awareness. When athletes develop awareness around their thinking, they open up endless possibilities. Journals are powerful tools of reference that can be used to create awareness and track negative thoughts. Athletes can begin to see their achievements and reflect on how their hard work has paid dividends. They can also identify strategies that work and those that do not.

Building Your Network. For athletes, surrounding themselves with the right people is essential. Having a coach, trainer, or training partner who is willing to seek advice from others, swallow their pride, apologize, and try new strategies is essential. In this chapter, we learned about specialists that can help athletes learn about the brain and how it powers and limits the human body. It gives us the ability to fuel that power and peel back those limits.

Believing in Yourself. Confidence is not about

knowing it all or a trait that you have but is something that you work hard to create. Being confident is the certainty that you can accomplish anything you set your mind and energy to. By fostering maturity and overcoming insecurity, confidence helps athletes handle relationship conflicts with teammates, trainers, and coaches, as well as solve problems that arise.

ONE LAST THING BEFORE YOU GO...

I would love to hear your feedback about this book—I personally read every single review!

If you have three minutes to help me out, can you please post a short review on Amazon or on the platform from where you purchased this book.

Thank you for your continued support.

- Hadley Mannings

REFERENCES

Clary, C. (2014, February 22). *Olympians use imagery as mental training.* New York Times. www.nytimes.com/2014/02/23/sports/olympics/olympians-use-imagery-as-mental-training.html

Cohn, P. (n.d.). *Sports visualization: the secret weapon of athletes.* Peak Performance Sports. https://www.peaksports.com/sports-psychology-blog/sports-visualization-athletes/

Griffin, M. (n.d.). *Can sleep improve your athletic performance?* https://www.webmd.com/fitness-exercise/features/sleep-athletic-performance

Guglielmo, C. (2015, July 7). *Finding an edge: gold medalist Lindsey Vonn talks tech.* CNET Magazine. https://www.cnet.com/news/finding-an-edge-gold-medalist-lindsey-vonn-talks-tech/

Irwin, C., Scorniaenchi, J., Kerr, N., Eisenmann, J. &

Feltz, D. (2012, May 11). *Aerobic exercise is promoted when individual performance affects the group: a test of the Kohler motivation gain effect.* Springer Link. https://link.springer.com/article/10.1007/s12160-012-9367-4

Jones, A. (2020, May 9). *Olympic gymnast Aly Raisman eats a mostly plant-based diet these days.* Women's Health. https://www.womenshealthmag.com/food/a32303743/aly-raisman-diet/

Kent, R. (2014). *Learning from athletes' writing: creating activity journals.* https://secure.ncte.org/library/NCTEFiles/Resources/Journals/EJ/1041-sep2014/EJ1041Learning.pdf

Macey, B. (n.d.). *How to eat like a professional athlete.* Select Health. https://selecthealth.org/blog/2016/06/how-to-eat-like-an-athlete

MacKenzie, D. (2015, April 13). *How Jordan Spieth won the masters with his mental game.* Golf State of Mind. https://golfstateofmind.com/jordan-spieths-mental-game/

Mustard, E. (2015, October 1). *Jets taking 350 rolls of toilet paper to London.* Sports Illustrated. https://www.si.com/extra-mustard/2015/10/01/new-york-jets-toilet-paper-london

National Sleep Foundation. (2020). *Seven sports stars who get plenty of zzz's.* Sleep.org https://www.sleep.org/articles/athletes-and-sleep/

O'Connor, B. (2015, April 28). *BU netminder proves mentality is key for hockey goalies at all levels.* Sports Illustrated. https://www.si.com/edge/2015/04/28/hockey-goalies-mental-toughness-bu-matt-oconnor

Other Live. (2018, July). *Tony Robbins: the power of positive thinking*. [Video]. YouTube. https://www.youtube.com/watch?v=5lqSCwzzm6U

Petre, A. (2019, July 23). *Tom Brady diet review: weight loss, meal plan, and more.* Healthline. https://www.healthline.com/nutrition/tom-brady-diet#bottom-line

Pioneer Billie Jean King moved the baseline for women's tennis. (2014, January 31). NPR. https://www.npr.org/2014/01/31/269423125/pioneer-billie-jean-king-moved-the-baseline-for-womens-tennis

Price-Mitchell, M. (2018, March 14). *Goal-Setting is linked to higher achievement.* Psychology Today. https://www.psychologytoday.com/us/blog/the-moment-youth/201803/goal-setting-is-linked-higher-achievement

Robbins, T. (n.d.). *Change your words, change your life.* https://www.tonyrobbins.com/mind-meaning/change-your-words-change-your-life/

Sports Psychology. (2020). American Psychological Association. https://www.apa.org/ed/graduate/specialize/sports

Toland, S. (2014, May 16). *Giants RB Rashad Jennings's dorky diet.* Sports Illustrated. https://www.si.com/edge/2014/05/16/giants-rb-rashad-jenningss-dorky-diet

Ward, M. (2017, June 28). *Tony Robbins: use this 4-step strategy to achieve any goal.* CNBC. https://www.cnbc.com/2017/06/28/tony-robbins-use-this-4-step-strategy-to-achieve-any-goal.html

Williams, A. (n.d.). *8 successful people who use the*

power of visualization. MBG Mindfulness. https://www.mindbodygreen.com/0-20630/8-successful-people-who-use-the-power-of-visualization.html

Writing Athletes. (n.d.). http://www.writingathletes.com/pro-athletes-write.html